JOHN KELLY was born in Enniskillen, County Fermanagh, in 1965. He is a freelance writer and broadcaster. His first novel, *Grace Notes and Bad Thoughts* (1994), was critically acclaimed. He divides his time between Enniskillen, Belfast and Dublin, where he works primarily for Radio Ireland.

A BLACKSTAFF PRESS PAPERBACK ORIGINAL

Cool about the ankles

JOHN KELLY

THE
BLACKSTAFF
PRESS
BELFAST

First published in May 1997 by
The Blackstaff Press Limited
3 Galway Park, Dundonald, Belfast BT16 0AN, Northern Ireland
with the assistance of
The Arts Council of Northern Ireland

Reprinted August 1997

Typeset by Techniset Typesetters, Newton-le-Willows, Merseyside

Printed in Ireland by ColourBooks Limited

A CIP catalogue record for this book
is available from the British Library

ISBN 0-85640-591-4

for
Lily and Tommy Kelly

Consider the grass growing
As it grew last year and the year before,
Cool about the ankles like summer rivers
When we walked on a May evening through the
meadows ...

from 'Consider the Grass Growing'
PATRICK KAVANAGH

1

Wycliffe Gordon shook the spit out of his trombone and nodded.

— I wanna play a special piece of music now ... and I wanna dedicate it to my Irish brother sitting right over here.

I nodded back humbly, and as I raised my glass in grateful benediction, he began. The sound was at once both unrecognisable and familiar and the nearby tables looked over at me for a clue. I tried to look knowledgeable, nodding and smiling and making a snaky kind of motion with my neck, trying to demonstrate that at least I was into the rhythm of it. Slow and inside out.

And then gradually the tune emerged like some strange

script clearing in my mind. A hackneyed, hammered, battered old tune was here being transformed into something light and curling like the smoke from a Marlboro. It was 'Danny Boy' and here in the Village Vanguard in New York City, Wycliffe Gordon was playing a solo and it was directed right at me – John Kelly, Fermanagh man. The music went through me, inside me, all over me, and spread the happiest sort of melancholy through every nerve and vein. I could have cried, laughed and half-cried. Instead I just sat back, stared at my glass, and breathed deeply through my nose.

And then as 'Danny Boy' spiralled to a close, the last note became nothing but breath and then a pure and heavy silence. After a few seconds we snapped out of it and the applause came – warm, genuine, generous applause. Wycliffe nodded over at me, I nodded back, and the band reappeared, Wessell Anderson shaking his glistening head in tribute.

I was at the bar with Lorraine Gordon, who runs the place, and was being well looked after by Tom Dillon the barman.

— Have one on me, Tom?

— I won't have a drink *on* you, thanks. But I'll have one *with* you.

— *Sláinte*.

Lorraine talked about her late husband Max Gordon and about Coltrane and Mingus and Sonny Rollins. I imagined them all in the room, on that stage. Dinah Washington in a blonde wig. Leadbelly's shiny socks. Miles being weird in the kitchen and Dizzy looking cool, the belt of his trousers hitched up under his oxters.

The band played three sets and I was the happiest man on the eastern seaboard. Between sets they hung around the bar and Wessell Anderson beamed.

— Hey! They call me Warmdaddy!

— All right, Warmdaddy, whaddya havin'?

— Just some water, please. Where you from?

— Ireland.

— Holland?

— No, Ireland.

— Oh, you the guy he played 'Danny Boy' for?

— Yeah, that's me.

— It's real beautiful there, right?

— It is surely, I said.

— It surely is, agreed Tom.

— I'm sure it is, added Lorraine.

— But come ye back, sang Wycliffe, when summer's in the m-e-ead-ow ...

And I thought to myself how much I used to hate that tune. I realised I was in one of those rare moments of absolute joy. Romance and reality had come together because this was New York, the imaginative hinterland, and this was the Village Vanguard. It was late and the music was hitting me right in the heart and nothing else mattered. I phoned Catherine and tried to explain. Apparently I made little sense.

Outside, the blizzard of '96 was blizzarding. People were skiing on Seventh Avenue. The amber lights of snow-ploughs flashed everywhere and huge drifts of snow were piling up on the sidewalk. There wasn't a snowball's chance of a cab home, so I walked around to Small's for more jazz. I felt bulletproof. It would take more than damp shoes and Rudi Giuliani to stop me.

Eventually I got the only cab in New York. The driver was from Senegal and was even more bewildered by the blizzard than I was.

— Never bee-for! he shouted.

— Never again! I shouted back.

— Yez sir, never ah-gin!

The street signs were caked in snow and you couldn't see your finger as we crawled uptown.

— Ah been een America since two month – never bee-for snow.

— You like Youssou N'Dour? I asked.

— My favourite!

— Game ball! I roared.

And I knew that as long as the World Trade Center was behind us that we were heading in the right direction. He hadn't a notion where he was going and I became the ignorant, omnipotent navigator. I shouted directions and he sang children's songs in a wonderful light and very musical voice. As we finally got to midtown Manhattan in a virtual white-out, I was singing 'The Holy Ground' and he was doing his best with 'Fine girl y'are'.

I got out somewhere on Lexington and tramped the rest of the way through the sort of snow I used to want for Christmas. It was freezing hard. The wind was howling and the snow lashed against my cheeks.

— Terrible night, said the night porter.

— It would lift ye! I agreed.

— Have a good night, sir?

— Ah don't be talkin'!

I was in New York to clear the head and to clear it for a purpose. One week to relax, go buck mad and work out how to write a book about what it was like to be thirty years old in 1996 and to have lived all your life in a place called Northern Ireland. I suspected that some distance might be the best policy – away from the place itself and

away from the baggage of work and worry. I wanted to
think about what I had been asked to do and work out
what there was to be said.

A week was nowhere near enough but I reckoned that a
week in New York was as good as six months anywhere
else and so here I was. Maybe this could be a way of
looking at where I was now and where I had been in 1965
and where and when I could meet myself in the middle as I
travelled, as usual, from two different directions. I could
travel in space, time, memory, location and speculation
and be a regular Dr Who.

Room service arrived with another omelette. Every
channel was devoted to the weather emergency. THE
BLIZZARD OF '96 was flashing across the screen and brave
reporters were angled into the wind like Arctic explorers
and screaming that it was total white-out and to stay
indoors. Looked like I had picked the best possible time to
come to New York City. Stranded, snowed in for ever –
and the thought was strangely exciting.

And then the job in hand – simply to think. Like a hermit
on top of his tower with everything and nothing on his
mind. Hotel stationery. File block. Omelette. Radio playing
Little Willie John, the Ronettes and Chet Baker. Snow
piling up on my thirty-fifth-floor windowsill and the sirens
beginning to wail below – just perfect for contemplating
Enniskillen, County Fermanagh, in 1965 and putting some
shape on thirty years in a place called Northern Ireland in a
world neither rural nor urban and yet a little of both. Some
discipline and forehead-rubbing focus and soon the
frustrations and delights of imperfect memory ...

I was marching up and down the garden pretending to be
a pipe band. Wrapped in a tartan blanket, my elbow

squeezed away at nothing and a dreadful, lazy, tuneless and vaguely Scottish siren lamented out from between my clenched teeth. Maybe it was 'Scotland the Brave' or 'We're All Off to Dublin in the Green' or 'The Sash' or 'Kelly, the Boy from Killane'. Whatever it was, Blackie McManus was going clean mad.

I was three years old and happy as the day was long. Fearless king of my own walled and unassailable kingdom – 28 Sedan Terrace, Enniskillen, the house where I lived for four years with my mother and my father and my Aunty Babby, who wore her silver hair in a bun, and was Daddy's aunty too. I'm sure the three of them were in the kitchen laughing at me – the cub – tramping up and down – left! right! left! right! – and this ferocious, diabolic howling and screeching banshee-wailing over the roof tops. In my head I could hear drums and marching feet.

Before that I can remember very little other than contentment and the smell of lino and wool. I was very happy, charmed to be taken for walks by all the Burns girls and Mary Campling and the only thing I was afraid of was dogs – except for Blackie McManus, who wouldn't touch you anyway. Sandie Shaw was always on the radio, and Dusty Springfield too.

I remember fireworks at Halloween – coloured discs like hard fried eggs nailed against a plank in the back yard. I remember our first television set and its little spaceman antennae aerial and the first wobbling picture of a black athlete limbering up and steadying himself in the starting blocks. I remember having the measles and wearing Aunty Peggy's sunglasses with the yellow, bubbly plastic rims and Granny bringing me the *Beano* annual and the smell of its new colourful pages. And the toy animals I played with – lions and tigers and rhinos and giraffes and elephants –

everything put in the crib at Christmas even though I knew there was only a cow and a donkey and sheep. Father Mullan laughed.

— Sure who knows *what* was in the crib? he said.

One day Paddy Kelly took me to Mulhern's, a gleaming palace of a place with shiny bottles and a warm smell. And then a robin built a nest on the saddle of my daddy's bicycle and he had to walk to work, the biscuit tin under his arm. Aunty Babby was old and took snuff and gave me money and we would throw dishcloths at each other for sport. She was always boiling priddies and prodding them with a knife. I said 'Hickory Dickory Dock' at my birthday party, bribed by a white chocolate mouse. I remember the black clothes of Mrs O'Doherty, who always minded me when my mother went up to communion, and how she would point at the picture of Our Lady of Perpetual Succour and I thought 'succour' was a funny word.

My mammy often told me I looked like the Wreck of the Hesperus and sometimes she said that I was like a weasel. She was called Lily and she used to be called Kennedy, which was my granny's name. She took me up the town every morning and she talked to God in the chapel. She put a mantilla on her head and cleaned my face with a handkerchief. If I needed to have a wee-wee she took me down Peggy the Bull's Lane. When I asked her what age she was, she always said she was twenty-one.

My favourite place was the coal house and whenever it rained I loved to shelter there and watch the rain bubble on the flagstones. The coal house was cosy and a sudden breeze made me shiver in a nice sort of way. I could have crouched there for hours looking out of the darkness like a scaldie in a nest, secure and yet open to the very weather and the wet brick and slate.

— Come in out of there, my mother would say, you'll get your death.

And then one afternoon the curly black-haired four-year-old head of Nigel Johnston appeared over the wall.

— Hi you, c'mere! he called.

Nigel Johnston was one of my friends and he lived away out in the country somewhere. His father was a farmer and his mother had a red face. Every day Nigel came to visit his granny a few doors up from us and we used to talk to each other over the wall. He had been to my birthday party where he and Trevor Armstrong had grabbed the best party hats and played soldiers all day – diving on the carpet and crawling around on their bellies shouting about commandos and all the time spitting machine-gun noises at each other from behind the chairs. I remember my mother asking them not to be so rough.

— Hi John, c'mere I wantye!

I silenced the pipes and ran down the garden to silently face him over the wall – him in his bright blue jumper and me draped in the rug. Suddenly he reared up and asked with great drama:

— Are you a *Prodesan* or a *Catlick*?

Was I what? What was a Prodesan? What was a Catlick? Was I one of them things? Maybe it was a trick question? Maybe I was both? Maybe I was neither? I didn't know what to say and for a moment I thought of crying. The garden and the coal shed and the wall and Nigel Johnston's bright blue jumper began to wheel around me and I tried to focus on the little cut-out patterns on my sandals. What was the answer to such a question? What bizarre new world was this? I thought for a moment and tried very hard to work out some kind of response. To say nothing would be stupid so I offered the only response I could manage.

— I'm a boy!

Understandably, Nigel Johnston's awakening Primary One bigotry wasn't satisfied.

— Don't be a dumbo, he hissed. What are you?

— I'm a boy! I'm a boy! I'm John Kelly and I'm a boy!

Prior to Nigel Johnston's sectarian interrogation, all I needed to know was the carpet and the linoleum of 28 Sedan Terrace and a thing called a Tan-Sad for going up the town. I knew my name was John and it was spelt JHON. My second name was Kelly and one day Mrs Maguire next door taught me to spell it: KELY. When I proudly wrote my whole name on my blackboard with scratchy purple chalk, I thought I had conquered all knowledge – my name, where I lived and what age I was. And soon by some strange process I found out that Nigel Johnston was a Prodesan and that I was a Catlick as well as being a boy. And then I knew that Prodesans had curly black hair and wore bright blue jumpers and that they called their mothers Mummy instead of Mammy.

On Saturday mornings I went up the town with my daddy, which is what my father was called, not dad, which is what the Prodesans said. They also said dad in the *Beano* so I knew that Dennis the Menace and Plug and all the Bash Street Kids must be Prodesans too. Their dads always hit them with big slippers but my daddy never did that.

When my daddy took me to the barber's I was lifted onto a board placed across the big red leather and chrome chair. Mr Campbell the barber stamped his foot and the chair rose higher until I was helpless and at his mercy. The whole procedure seemed mysterious and pointless to me but it was fascinating in its way and the big mirror let me see what I looked like – and I looked exactly like a boy. No two ways about it. Big, big ears – just like my daddy. When

Mr Campbell had finished snipping and shearing he would wet a comb and part my hair at the side with great precision. That's the way big men combed their hair and the part had to be on the left, but in the mirror it was on the right, which was the hand you blessed yourself with and held a knife. Sometimes for a treat Mr Campbell would ask me to point out one of the colourful bottles on the shelf and in a flash he would pour some of the mysterious liquid first onto his hands and then all over my head.

— There you are, he would say, you smell like a rose.

After the barber's, myself and my father went to the Island. My father was a tall man and he wore a straight greeny-coloured raincoat and a cap. He didn't walk as fast as my mother and he never cleaned my face with a handkerchief. On Saturday mornings he looked very different to when he came home from work during the week with sawdust in his hair. Sometimes he had a donkey jacket and a yellow helmet. He washed it all away on Friday night, and on Saturday all he wanted to do was to go up the town with me and go to the Island. He was a carpenter and Jesus' father was a carpenter too. My father was called Tommy Kelly and Jesus' father was called Joseph Christ. His back yard in Nazareth was full of boards and planks and saws and chisels and hammers and mallets and awls. The kitchen floor was covered in sawdust and when he came home for his dinner Mary would gently hold his hand and pick the splinters out of his fingers with a needle. Jesus was a good boy and did what his mother and father told him – although Joseph was only his foster father and his real father was God, who was everybody's father. Jesus was God too (even when he was a wee boy) and the Holy Ghost was God as well.

Every bright early evening all my workings-out were verified and reinforced by the prayers my mother said with me. You had to say your prayers every morning and every night and thank God for everything. In the name of the Father and of the Son and of the Holy Ghost. Amen.

Outside Nigel Johnston was shouting about commandos and a late blackbird was singing on the coal house roof. Inside, all washed and shiny under the cool sheets, I chanted back.

— God bless Mammy, God bless Daddy, God bless Aunty Babby, God bless Granny, God bless Nana, God bless Aunty Peggy, God bless Mr Campbell, God bless Nigel Johnston, God bless Mrs Maguire, God bless Trevor Armstrong, God bless all the Burnses, God bless Mary Campling and God bless Blackie McManus.

And then the final prayer, always uttered with great, triumphant and yawning satisfaction:

— And – God – bless – me!

2

This snowy morning I prayed that cabs would be running, that the Museum of Modern Art would be open, that Woody Allen would be playing in Michael's on Monday night, that I wouldn't get my head in my hands in Brooklyn, that my shoes would dry out and that Stars deli was still there – and it was. And so to breakfast to drink the coffee and eat the ham and eggs and talk the second language to Maria: over easy, sunnyside up. To take my rightful place at the chrome counter and hunch up over the yellowy glass of cold, cold water.

As Maria shrugged once more about the weather, the waiters stared out the window and complained happily in Spanish about the last time there was a blizzard like this.

When I told them I was here for a whole week they
laughed and grimaced and said they were sorry.

But I was delighted with myself – the place was
beautiful. Outside it was as silent as a winter morning on
the Forthill. Redwings and thrushes and robins hopping
their little constellations in the snow, the odd squeal of a
child, but other than that, nothing – a comfortable and total
silence. It was eerie. Happed-up people walked the very
centre of the avenue where the snow had been slightly
cleared and gone was the constant flowing blur of yellow
cabs and ornate trucks. Gone were the horns and their
sudden unexpected harmonies. Gone was the siren and
chase and the waiter shook his head and shouted *whoah!* as
a reckless posse of skiers whooshed past.

— More coffee, Irishman? asked Maria.

— Sure, Maria, *gracias*.

— *De nada*.

New York. Ratification. Realisation. Re-creation. Saying
gracias, talking about bucks and chilli in a bowl – and far
from where I was reared. A few bucks for breakfast, a few
bucks for Maria, and a walk up to Fifth Avenue, right up
the middle of snowdrift Fifth Avenue. Frith's Alley and my
grandmother watching *Easter Parade* on the television.

Fred Astaire was steppin' out with his baby and we sat
with cups of tea and Marie biscuits. My mother and father
enjoyed the dancing – 'A Couple of Swells' and 'Drum
Crazy'. Fred Astaire was only in the film because Gene
Kelly had hurt his ankle and we all agreed that Astaire
wasn't as good as Kelly but he was a terror anyway
because he had nothing much going for him. My grandmother loved all the Easter bonnets and suddenly
announced that someone belonging to us lived on Fifth
Avenue, walked on that very pavement – this very

pavement – these very flagstones – where the whole style was promenading to the sounds of Irving Berlin. It seemed more than an ocean from our small and quiet living room to here – Fifth Avenue, Manhattan, New York City, America, and a mysterious big-eared Kelly waving out from a skyscraper apartment in the next parish.

I scanned the towering creamy-white apartment blocks and the thousands of windows and wondered if there was someone up there who looked like me. Big-eared, lanky paleface – an El Greco stretch with a new spring in his step – trying to do his New York walk in three feet of fresh snow. The sun was dazzling and the echoing notes of a sax player filled the perfect acoustic outside Saks. Up in the Waldorf, Cole Porter was still in his smoking jacket, gazing out the window at the eiderdown of snow on Cuilcagh mountain.

And Luke Kelly was singing:

Tell me who is that giant with the gold curling hair,
He who rides at the head of the band?
Seven feet in his height with some inches to spare
And he looks like a king in command!
Ah my lads, that's the pride of the bold Shelmaliers,
'Mong our greatest of heroes, a man!
Fling your beavers aloft and give three ringing cheers
For John Kelly, the Boy from Killane!

It was a song with my name in it. And it made my feet tap and my spine shiver. John Kelly – foremost of all in the grim Gap of Death. Luke belted it out and its martial power was infectious. I heard it on the wireless, the reassuring sound of Radio Éireann drifting up from the midlands:

For the boys march at morn from the South to the North,
Led by Kelly, the Boy from Killane!

And then suddenly:

— Don't be singing that – you'll be lifted!

Lifted? What did *that* mean? I thought I knew what *lifted* meant: lifted by the hair, or sometimes when it was cold Babby would say that it would lift you outside and the wind would go through you. But what had being lifted got to do with my song? Bewildered again, I stopped singing about somebody called John Kelly from Killane.

It was Nigel Johnston who taught me 'The Sash'. It must have been him. It mentioned Enniskillen and someplace called *Derryogerrim* and the Boyne and it was a good tune too. I stopped singing that as well just in case I would be lifted but Nigel Johnston stamped on proud and fearless.

— They'll not lift me – my uncle's a B Special.

I thought about bees and buzzing.

— What's a B Special? I asked.

— A Prodesan, he replied. It was old but it was bee-yoo-dee-ful and the colours . . .

Then I got briefly brave, thinking I wouldn't be lifted if I was with Nigel Johnston and his uncle a B Special – whatever that was.

Fling your beavers aloft and give three ringing cheers
For John Kelly, the Boy from Killane!

There was nothing in those lines to betray its '98 rebellious content, but Nigel Johnston had already developed some kind of detector. He took a mad swipe of a guess.

— That's one of them friggin' rebel songs!

— What's a friggin' rebel?

— A Catlick.

And then later in the scullery.

— Aunty Babby? Are Catlicks friggin' rebels?

— Who did you hear talkin' like that?

— Nigel Johnston says that Prodesans are B Specials and Catlicks are friggin' rebels and that –

— Don't be saying words like that.

— What words?

— That word ... f——

— F——? B Special? F Special?

Nigel Johnston must have had a similarly confused conversation in his farmhouse kitchen out the road, but his oracle had clearly been more forthcoming. Next day, at the garden wall, he had a few more facts for me.

— Catlicks are fuckin' rebel bastards, he said calmly. Croppies lie down!

I was a very bewildered boy. Catlicks, Prodesans, Croppies, B Specials, rebels and then three words – fuckin', friggin' and bastards – that I was not allowed to say. Maybe if I said them I'd be lifted? In any case I didn't say them – and I kept my eye out for the B Specials.

In July it was time for the bands and they marched up and down past the house. They were practising for a big day called the Twelfth and I couldn't wait because the bands were big and noisy and colourful and they had bagpipes. Nigel Johnston talked about it for weeks and he swaggered about the garden, throwing a brush handle into the air and catching it. I mimicked this spectacular activity and turned out to be more skilled at it than he was. That didn't please him.

— You'll not be there anyway, he growled.

— I will, I said, I seen the bands last year up the town.

— It's only for Prodesans. Croppies lie down!

— I'm not a Croppy!

— You friggin' are, so you are!

(I didn't know whether I was one or not.)

On the Twelfth I could hear the drums and I wanted to see the bands up the town.

— A soldier in King James's army was about to shoot oul' King Billy, Babby said, and James kicked the gun out of his hand and shouted 'Don't shoot that man and leave my daughter a widow.' And then the Protestants bate the Catholics.

— The Prodesans bate the Catlicks?

— Aye. It was a big battle and the Protestants bate the Catholics and that's the Protestants celebrating up the town now. Do you not hear all the bangin'?

— When was the battle?

— Ah now, she sighed, it wasn't the day or yesterday.

— What's a Fenian?

— Who did you hear talkin' like that?

I went out into the back yard and shivered in the black cave of the coal house. I didn't want to go to the parade any more. I was a Catlick and Nigel Johnston was a Prodesan and the Prodesans bate the Catlicks in a big battle and Nigel Johnston was glad and he was up the town now, celebrating with the B Specials. All the Catlicks were at home. Even Blackie McManus was in the house – afraid of being lifted.

3

In his book-lined West Fifty-fourth Street apartment
William Rossa Cole was sipping a Bloody Mary. Bill is a
warm, welcoming and literary man and, among other
things, is the grandson of Jeremiah O'Donovan Rossa, one
of the longest beards in Irish history, well commemorated
by a gigantic erratic at the entrance to St Stephen's Green.
Whenever we meet he talks about Chet Baker and I ask
him about James Baldwin.

— He sat right in that chair you're sitting in now. He
was a sweet guy. Stayed here a lot.

I speculate, too, about the Belfast man who suddenly
appears like another erratic in one of Baldwin's novels. Bill
can't remember who it was but I like to think it might well

have been the same Belfast man who introduced us in the first place, David Hammond – *chanteur d'Irlande du Nord* as he is described in the footnotes to the French Heaney. ('Davey! Did you ever hear Big Bill Broonzy?' 'Aye! I used to live in his house in Chicago.')

I was definitely born too late. When everyone in Europe was romanticising about New York and the bohemia of Greenwich Village, people like Bill Cole were there in the thick of it. As I wander around Bleecker Street, still hoping to find the remnants of something, I realise again that much of my experience is well out of time, out of context, and out of place. For instance, Bill's first sight of Bob Dylan was not at Slane Castle on the banks of the Boyne but rather when the lad Zimmerman was cycling through the crowds in Washington Square. Someone pointed him out as the new guy who was playing in the White Horse. The Clancys were there too – and David Hammond.

I examined the bookshelves and reported the news from home. Everyone in New York had caring questions. Yes, there was a peace and it had lasted a long time. It was wonderful. Belfast was finally buzzing. Riverdance. It could never ever go back now. Never. It couldn't. Even so, everyone was getting a bit worried because nothing much was happening politically as far as anybody could see. Ordinary people were being asked to take huge, generous and imaginative leaps and, indeed, were doing so. The politicians, we agreed, were making a hames of it. Clouds gathered.

In a surreal interlude Bill dug out a long-player of Micheál Mac Liammóir reciting Pearse's panegyric at the grave of O'Donovan Rossa and the words 'shall never be at peace' were ominous and startling.

— Don't let anyone hear you playing that, I joked

nervously. You'll be lifted!

I gazed out the window at the snow falling on the traffic on Seventh Avenue. I was holding the gold-topped cane of O'Donovan Rossa in my hand and was trying hard to get my head back into New York. Up on the roof, Bill's son Rossa took my picture. It was blizzarding hard and he stood me in the same spot where Jimmy Baldwin had been photographed looking down on the matchbox cars and ant people of Seventh Avenue. It was grey, half-snowing, half-raining, and mysterious. The snow was up to my knees and Rossa said he'd make me look like James Dean and then he'd drive me to Brooklyn. He succeeded only in the latter.

Many floors below me, the Carnegie deli was buzzing with orders for pastrami and tales of fabulous balloon-folding acts and Danny Rose stories to beat all Danny Rose stories. It has become a cliché to compare New York City to a film set, but that's exactly what it is. In fact New York is more than a film set, it is also a movie star. Name check. *42nd Street, Breakfast at Tiffany's, Taxi Driver, Escape from New York, On the Town, The Belle of New York, King Kong, The Prisoner of Second Avenue, New York, New York, Sweet Smell of Success, Manhattan, Annie Hall* et cetera, et cetera.

Back in the hotel, I looked up Kelly in the New York phone book.

— Nothin' only Kellys, my grandmother said. They're everywhere – even in Amerikay.

The name comes from Ceallach and the Kellys were once kings of Galway. Our connection arrived in from Donegal, two big-eared brothers rattling over the clay roads with a horse and cart. They were tailors, but this was all so far back that nobody knew anything for sure. Townies didn't bother about genealogy because they owned nothing – no farm of land, no homestead – and what's more, their immediate history was one of famine, emigration, consumption, unemployment and cannon fodder. A regal lineage meant nothing when it was only the ones who had gone away who were doing well. Gene Kelly, Grace Kelly and De Forrest Kelley from *Star Trek* – the first Kelly in space. Then there was John Kelly who stole a pig and was transported to Australia for his sins. His son was called Ned and he robbed banks with a bucket on his head. Seán T. O'Kelly – president of Ireland. Then there was a man called Oisín Kelly who was a sculptor and a Prodesan too. 'On Mother Kelly's Doorstep' was on the wireless and Mrs Maguire used to sing through the hedge:

— Has anybody here seen Kelly? K E double L Y?

Granda Kelly was dead and he was in heaven, which was in the sky. He used to work in Mulhern's and he was very gentle. He smoked Woodbines and backed horses and played the bones. My daddy said that he had beautiful handwriting and that he never ever said a bad word. Granda's wife was my Nana Kelly and she had a big chest and she laughed and sang sad, quiet songs to herself. She used to put ice cream into lemonade and tell me that I was a good cub. She was called Ellen but some people called her Nelly. I thought Nelly Kelly was a very funny name. Granda Kelly was called Richard and some people called him Dickie. Aunty Babby was his sister.

Before Sedan Terrace the Kellys lived in Gas Lane or Frith's Alley. It was entered through a kind of Jaffa Gate from the Gaol Square and ran parallel to Belmore Street. The Orrs lived in the first house and they were cousins of the Kellys. Then there was the Hyneses, the Maguires, the Kellys, James Orr's workshop, the McCuskers and the McKernans. The Back of the Bricks. The Bowery.

James was a cartwright and he lived with the Kellys. He made carts and cartwheels and he once met the devil down the lough. He said that the devil was wearing a black coat with a velvet collar and he often told my father that Velvetcollar would get him. When he cut himself with a chisel or an adze he would scrape an old dusty cobweb from the rafters and slap it over the cut. The dirtier the cobweb, the better. He had very big ears.

And then there was Paddy Kelly who shot the brass knobs off the end of his bed for sport. He was a sailor and he played the harmonica and his mother and father died in a flu epidemic and were buried together on the same day. That was the most frightening thing I had ever heard and only Paddy's own heroic legend could banish that nightmare thought. My father often told me about him, happily repeating tales he knew to be untrue. How Paddy sailed with the convoys and once fired a shell straight up into the air and shelled his own ship. Exotic names like Cape Spartivento and Mussolini suddenly widened the world and there were photographs to prove it all. Paddy in his uniform – bell bottoms and wide collar and HMS *Victory* written on his cap. And the one of Paddy and another happy sailor dancing a sedentary hornpipe on a depth charge. On the back it said, 'Spider and Windy, Malta 1943'.

It seemed, also, that during the war Paddy's legend needed a better source; Frith's Alley wasn't nearly glamorous enough. On envelopes from around the world there suddenly appeared a new address: Paddy Kelly, Frith *Avenue*, Enniskillen.

Paddy married a Geordie and lived in Jarrow in the north-east of England and one time he and his wife came over to Ireland and brought a Geordie friend with them

called John Walker. John told me that his father had been
on a big march when poor starving people had walked
from Jarrow to London. They were, he said, the working-
class people of the north of England. My father agreed that
they were great people to walk the whole way to London,
and they had nothing going for them – no jobs and they
were hungry.

The weekend of their visit, my father put me on his
shoulders and we all plashed up the stream and through
the rushes to the Mill Lough. I gathered bulrushes to bring
home. Paddy caught a pike and said it was a trout. And I
believed him. My father's people had all fished. A stretch
of water was baited with blue clay and yellow meal and
lines were set. The Kellys fished at the Post Office, an
outcrop of land with a telegraph pole on it across from
Killyhevlin, and they hauled in huge bronze bream to be
salted and hung up. With spoonbaits and spinners, they
hooked perch and pike. Eels were good, too, and they
jumped about in the pan.

Townies did what they could to feed their families – the
Wall Street Crash, the Hungry Thirties, the Depression.
People took in washing, worked at their trades, did casual
jobs, had their own odd schemes, and as the thirties came
to a bloody close, many more got blown to smithereens, as
they always had, in the many and various regiments of the
British Army. And Babby said:

Some of them had boots and stockings,
Some of them had nothing at all,
Some of them had big bare asses,
Coming back from the Crimean War.

My mother's people were Kennedys and they used to
live in Eden Street. It ran down from the Diamond and it

used to be called Pudding Lane. Eden after paradise. Adam and Eve. Our first father and mother and the devil and the apple and the rib and the angel with the sword. My Granda Kennedy was a baker and he worked in a white cloud of flour in Whaley's in Paget Square, but he was in heaven now, just like Granda Kelly. And then Granny lived in Derrin Road with my Aunty Peggy and the house always smelt of baking and briquettes. It was full of holy statues and there was a dish on the wall with a picture of John F. Kennedy and his wife Jackie, who was beautiful. Granny said President Kennedy was a good man and that he was her cousin. That meant he was related to me too – maybe a second cousin.

Saint Martin was a black man from Peru and some people said he was 'Sugar' Ray Robinson. Saint Jude was for hopeless cases and Saint Antony would find anything you had lost. One of the statues of Mary had holy water inside it and you had to screw off her crown to get it out. Granny used to splash it all over me on the way out the door.

— Mind yourself! Be good and be careful.

Aunty Peggy had a thing called arthritis and her hands were different to mine. She prayed all the time and watched *Coronation Street*. The slate roof tops, the chimney pots, the back yards, the cat, Ena Sharples, the Baird television and Brian Baird reading the news. I thought he owned the television because his name was on it. When Granny and Aunty Peggy watched the television they would sometimes gasp or laugh or sigh, 'ah, now'. Sometimes Peggy would make a face and say it was too loud and Granny would turn it off. They didn't like shouting or arguing or cowboys and Indians or war films.

— Nothin' only shootin'! Granny would say.

The granny's favourite word was 'gallivanting', and she was always complaining about people gallivanting round the country. Whenever she took me out for a walk she used to hold me by the hood of my anorak – and I hated that. Reined in. Halter and harness. She would point at the baby swans on the lough.

— Look at those wee swans. They do as they're bid.

I didn't know what that meant. And if I wanted to go near the water she would tell me that I would drown.

Granny came from Carrickmacross, which was in the Free State, but it wasn't Bundoran. Bundoran was the seaside. Carrickmacross, she said, was in the back of beyond – in the middle of nowhere. Sometimes she made lemonade for me out of lemons and sugar and kept it cold on the stone floor of the larder. She also gave me treacle on a spoon and one day she threw a bin lid at a mouse and killed it. Saint Martin used to be nice to mice and feed them but Granny said it was easy for him because he was a saint. She had hard skin on her knees and when I asked her what was wrong with them she always said, 'Too much prayin'.'

She had loads of brothers and sisters and they were my great-uncles and great-aunts. The men were all called Nolan, which was her name before she was Kennedy, and the women were all called different names because they were married. Jack Nolan had a small farm and lived up a mountain in Dowra, where he read books and wrote rhymes. Paddy Nolan was an electrician and he drank whiskey out of tiny glasses and told jokes and lived in Southampton which was in England. Lily Nolan was old and she could speak French and listen to the news in Irish. Peggy Conlon was good steam and she lived in Bray and she spoke Irish all the time. Agnes used to live in Glasgow and she had a boxer dog. Gertie lived in Riverside. Granny was called Rosie and she was the youngest. There had been many other brothers and sisters but they had all died. Their mother, my great-grandmother, was a dressmaker and her picture was on the sideboard. She looked like my Aunty Úna. Úna was Irish for Agnes and Agnes was Latin for lamb and she lived in Luton which was in a place called Beds and that was in England. Across the water. She left on a boat because Ireland was an island and Enniskillen was an island and the Island was an island too.

Such were the internal litanies and mantras about places and people and their relationships that slowly built up a picture of my world. Associations began to spread out and out, and more and more connections started to be made. Everything seemed to lead somewhere, perhaps to some discovery or revelation, to represent some neat progression from one little piece of knowledge to another and to put some shape on the chaotic and the unknowable.

Questions continued to shower like inescapable arrows from over the wall, and gradually I was beginning to learn the skills of living in a place called Northern Ireland – the North, the Six Counties, Ulster. Be careful what you say – better still, say nothing at all. Read signs, know your ground and crack the code. Already, by four years of age, my world was complex, and I was manoeuvring and negotiating my way through it. Nigel Johnston said that he wasn't my friend. I almost knew the reason why, and so, learning fast, I said nothing. It was 1969 when we moved to the new estate, Hillview. Babby immediately cobbled the sink with spuds and wiped the gleaming new draining board of stainless steel.

4

The television was wall-to-wall blizzard. Rudi Giuliani was ordering everybody to stay home. Emergency traffic only. It was like a Batman comic – disaster had struck Metropolis and the mayor, the chief of police and Batman were live on television promising to sort it out. The last time I was here, a native American stood before the United Nations and warned that not enough respect was being paid to Mother Nature. Almost immediately there was a tidal wave that nearly flooded Manhattan. Here again the great city of New York had been given a quare gunk and was suddenly at the mercy of an even greater force – tons of snow.

Stephen Rea was in town making movies and a crowd of

us went for a stroll in the crunchy snow of Central Park. It was beautiful, bright and glowing. Snow-boarders, skiers, skaters, and one clown in shorts and a pink vest who cycled round and round showing off his tan. As we walked across the frozen lake I looked up at the towering parkside apartments and sang 'The Sash Mia Farrow Wore'. Wintery snaps were taken, snowballs were thrown, exotic dogs were remarked upon, and someone proposed that were we all to crash through the ice, only Stephen would be mentioned in the *New York Times* and that the *Fermanagh Herald* might get around to me eventually. Group portrait at a sign that read: DANGER THIN ICE.

(I don't know very many movie stars but I met Sean Penn once. It was at a party which was already pretty surreal but took a further twist when he asked me did I know a certain public house in Lisnaskea.)

On freezing Saturday mornings after the snip, snip, snip of the cold blade across my forehead, my daddy folded his cap and slid it into his coat pocket like a gun. Reverently, we went through the entry into Frith's Alley and along and across Quay Lane and on down to the Island. The Island was a mysterious jungle of colours and shafts of insect-jewelled sun. Midges. Bluebottles. Daddy-longlegs. Red-brown corrugated iron sheds formed the hard rear rampart of an otherwise deep, cool, green enclosure where chestnut trees flung their huge palm-of-the-hand leaves on the ground. The biggest spiky chessies were always swinging out of reach and sometimes they plopped heavily in the lough and floated away like mines. Mines to sink Paddy's ship or James Orr out trolling with a spoon.

The Island was where my father played with his friends when he was a boy. Where they launched themselves on

makeshift cruises on cattle-cots. Where they climbed trees.
Where they shouted and screamed. Where they gathered
chessies and made slings and catapults and bows and
arrows. This is where they killed a song thrush dead.
Angels With Dirty Faces, Tom Sawyer and Huckleberry
Finn.

Under the East Bridge the water was deep and you
couldn't go near it or you'd be drowned. The old pike
floated steadily upwards and flashed an eye in the drifting
oily clouds. Bats hung upside down under the great stone
arches awaiting their long night of screeching over the
rushes and roofs and chimney pots. Bats were blind and
would get stuck in your hair. Dracula could turn into a bat
and he would suck your blood like the midges. But
sunlight was safe light and warm light and my father
hurled sticks up into the trees and down came the chessies
with heavy thuds on the soft fallen leaves. The ripe ones
exploded and split in all directions to reveal rich brown
jewels packed tight in the soft foamy bed, all shiny like the
granny's mahogany table. I gathered them up and stuffed
them in the ragged pockets of my anorak. Among them
would be the King of a Hundred. Another I would plant in
a jar and it would grow into an enormous chessie tree
beside our new pebble-dashed house.

I knew there were three hundred and sixty-five islands
in Lough Erne and there were three hundred and sixty-five
days in the year. But the Island was not a real island – not
for years had it been any class of an island at all. And yet
this place was still called the Island because it was the
Island of Ceithle or Inis Ceithleann or Enniskillen. The
town where I lived with my mother and father and my
Aunty Babby. Enniskillen was the biggest town in
Fermanagh and Fermanagh was in Ireland, which was a

small country in the Atlantic Ocean and it looked like a sideways dog.

Enniskillen was called after Ceithle, who was the wife of Balor of the Stout Blows. They were Formorians, who were by all accounts hard tickets – fierce pirate people who lived in Fermanagh long, long before Jesus was ever born in Bethlehem. After the great Battle of Moytura, Ceithle swam the length of Lough Erne and landed on the Island, where she died with her back against a chessie tree. The Island was then called after her and so was the town. 'Pistrix,' my mother said. But that's how Enniskillen got its name and that's the place where I lived. A market town in the North but near the border with the South.

The new estate wasn't finished yet and Mr Gallogly drove his dumper truck over the lunar landscape of his own tracks. My daddy pulled the dockens out of the garden and made a garden roller from an oil drum filled with concrete, which he used to flatten out the raw, wormy clay. Grass seed was scattered and a rambling rose, all ferocious purple thorns, was planted against the fence. But you couldn't plant a chessie tree. It would grow too big and you'd have to cut it down again.

The fireplace had a door on it and I worried about my first Christmas there and how Santy Claus would be defeated by this. 'Jiggered,' my father would say. I prayed to Saint Martin and Saint Jude and Saint Antony that Santy Claus would not be jiggered and would find another way in. Somebody said that he'd come in through the letter box. Letter box, me granny's pocket! I thought, and I anticipated Christmas with some gloom and despair.

But Santy Claus could not be beaten with a big stick and sure enough he arrived at Christmas with a cavalry fort. He even took the time to set it up for me. Cowboys down on one knee, each taking aim at a corner. Lookouts with rifles were scanning the horizon from the tower. The gate was open and a troop of neckerchiefed cavalry rode out across the carpet, led by a fiery general waving a curving sword. I spent the following year on my stomach, at eye level with cowboys and cavalry and their rearing-up horses, making all the noises of gunfire and death in the back of my throat.

I was a cowboy for several years. I got the suit – waistcoat, fringed trousers that were far too short, a hat, a sheriff's badge and two gleaming silver six-shooters in their ruby-studded holsters. An added detail was to use a whang to tie the bottom of the holster to my thigh. That's what the cowboys did in the movies, and it kept the guns from flying about as I galloped around the garden slapping my own backside with the palm of my hand.

My father taught me how to shoot him.

— Aaaggghhh, he groaned, you got me!

He would slap his hand to his heart and grimace, fall down on one knee, and then spin over onto his front. And I would half-laugh and watch in horror as he flipped violently onto his back, thrust his arms out along the floor and lay completely still. I blew across the barrels of the guns and spun them awkwardly on my fingers before sliding them back in their holsters without saying a word. The room was deadly quiet and I stood awaiting the next move. Nothing would happen for ages and then as I tiptoed over to his body he would suddenly leap up and start shooting and I would collapse, all laughter and tickles and screams.

— I got ya good, he would say.

Soon I learnt the names of Jesse James, Billy the Kid, Butch Cassidy and the Sundance Kid, Buffalo Bill, General

Custer and Little Big Horn. Geronimo, Crazy Horse, Apache, Arapaho and Cherokee. My favourite was Big Chief Sitting Bull, Chief of the Sioux. The next Christmas I asked Santy Claus for an Indian suit. I realised I had been on the wrong side.

5

I had met an old school friend and his wife on the plane out of Dublin. The flight was badly delayed and I was glad of the company. They were travelling home to New York with their baby son and immediately the stories started. Primary school, St Mick's, what's so and so doing? Did you hear about such and such? Teachers took a hammering – deservedly, we thought – and old injustices were rehearsed once more and sometimes laughed at.

Strange to be going to New York for a jaunt and to meet someone exactly my own age who was already living there, married, and a father. A reality sandwich to chew on in immigration. Someone who did the same spelling tests each morning and sat the same 11-plus, and although we had never been close friends, we had begun our day in exactly the same way for nearly fourteen years.

The plane was twelve hours late and I knew immediately that my first head-clearing exercise had been a failure. I would arrive exhausted, stressed out and ready to kill dead things. Too late for the gig as well. Otis Clay, soul singer. I was supposed to have gone straight there to meet Phast Phreddie Patterson – Neat Guy – from Warner Brothers. That was all out the window now and still to come was two hours at the carousel waiting for baggage I was convinced they had lost. It was three in the morning.

When I finally got through, cursing and whingeing, I said my farewells to my friends and their sleeping baby and stepped into a cab. It was stinking. It was New York – the bridge, the skyline, the river, the million glowing windows and the head suddenly opening up. Injection. Rush. Buzz. Immediate hit. Barry Flanagan's big bronze hares on Park Avenue were frozen mid-leap in the snow.

It's true that Americans return to Ireland in their thousands to find their roots, and it is also true that I cross the Atlantic in the other direction to find mine. In the odd embrace of Manhattan I find a weird and satisfying homecoming that proves to me my still half-baked, small-hours theory that we are all to some extent American. American well beyond the obvious conquest of our taste buds and viewing habits.

Certainly I grew up in what they call a small town, but in my own head I was just as urban as any city dweller. For all the fields and loughs around our estate, I still had a neighbourhood, I had my streets, street corners and wastelands. What's more, I had television, movies and comics – pretzels, Madison Square, hot dogs, sirens, hydrants, George M. Cohan, Broadway, Kojak and steam.

And so it is that an Enniskillen man can step into
Manhattan and wrap it around him and strut about the
place like he owns it. It is all exactly as he expects it and
presents a rare opportunity to dwell in his own imagination. To listen to McCoy Tyner in Sweet Basil. To be with
musicians on the night Dizzy Gillespie died. To play Artie
Shaw on the jukebox in P.J. Clarke's and pretend to be Ray
Milland. Lost weekend? Sure I had worse weekends than
that many's the time.

And then there's the other side to my American
hinterland, a side that's much harder to romanticise. On
the cheap ride of the Staten Island ferry, crossing back to
Manhattan, it is easy to see through the eyes of new
arrivals, full of hope and fear and half-dead from the
journey, praying that their destination would be a new
heaven and not another hell. The whole story so terrible
that it seems indulgent to tell it out loud. And it is exactly
this reality that elicits a certain guilt in a seven-hour flight
and a week in a midtown hotel. Not all the Kellys ended
up on Fifth Avenue waving down at Fred Astaire.

Going through immigration I had talked to my travelling
companions about living in New York. They liked it and
they didn't. They had a child to think about now, and the
thought of him going to St Michael's Primary in a duffel
coat in a place called Cornagrade was a rather more
comforting one.

I was in a room with lots of other boys and their mothers
and everybody was howling – even some of the mothers. I
only ever cried at the sight of my own blood or as a last
resort, as a signal that I had lost control, had given in, and
was helpless. It was a call to be rescued from whatever
circumstance it was I could no longer cope with. Crying

was a sign that I was genuinely in trouble and that my parents should rescue me. It changed the situation immediately and for the better. Tears were salty and once you started, it was hard to stop. Crying was all right but girnin' made your parents cross. Whingeing was worse.

I didn't cry on my first day at school. I was much too excited. For months beforehand, up the town with my mother, she would talk to her friends about me going to school and her friends would talk about their boys going to school. They would try to introduce us all to each other but we would just stare each other out and pull our mothers' arms to get away.

— And Peter's going to school in September too. He might be in the same class as you. Wouldn't that be nice?

I turned away and the other boy turned away. I didn't like the look of him. Nigel Johnston was supposed to be a nice boy too, and now he wouldn't play with me. And when I stopped saying 'God bless Nigel Johnston', my mother said that I should keep saying it because everybody was a child of God. So I said 'God bless Nigel Johnston' – but I didn't mean it.

This boy's mother had a stupid voice and just because she was my mother's friend, her dumpy wee boy didn't have to be my friend.

— Ah, he's shy, his mother said.

Buzz off! I thought. (I was getting cranky in my old age.)

Sure enough he was in my class, which was called Pee One, and he was bawling his eyes out. They were all bawling their eyes out. Big babies screaming as the classroom door closed on the straining faces of the mothers, jostling each other to get a last doleful look at their little boys. Mrs Martin smiled as she gently shut them out, and I began to look around me.

Pictures on the walls – big bright pictures of boys and
girls and dogs and cats and words and numbers. There
was a blackboard with coloured chalk. There was a tin bath
full of sand and another one with taps and plastic buckets
and funnels and containers and jars. In the corner there
was a table with chessies on it. Peter's mother had her face
pressed up against the window and was waving in at her
crybaby son. He was starting to girn and I thought he
should get a clip round the ear.

Mrs Martin arranged us around low square tables and
we sat on tiny wooden chairs. Patrick O'Doherty was the
smallest boy in the class and everyone wanted to sit beside
him. One boy began to pick his nose and, worse again, eat
what he had mined. Another boy's party trick was to pull
the hair clean out of his head. Stephen Curry could yodel.

Still smiling, Mrs Martin asked all of us our names and
wrote them on the board. I can still ramass off an imperfect
list of names: Aiden O'Callaghan, Martin Roche, Barry
Lynam, Mark McGowan, Cosmas Cassidy, Gerard
Sommers, Seamus Ferguson, Donal McGandy, Kevin
Watson, Michael Dunlop, Michael McAloon and Dermot
Gunn. Mrs Martin was very nice to us and soon everybody
had stopped crying except for Whinger.

When I ream off their names now it sounds to me like a
kind of a poem. Later on, anyone called Stephen became
Stevie, and anyone called Michael became Micky, and we
played in the playground and shinned up the poles of the
shelter. We wrestled and played tig and had piggyback
races. John Corrigan pretended he was Randolph Scott and
Ken Savage shouted, 'Ah-Oh Jungo!' The steps and railings
down into the playground became a fire engine and a man
walked past who looked like d'Artagnan. I decided that
school was a bit daft but there was nothing else for it but to

join in and buzz around the playground like a swarm of squealing bees.

After the break Mrs Martin looked serious.

— Who took the chestnuts? Put up your hand.

I put up my hand.

— Come up here, John Kelly.

I leapt up from my seat and stepped forward, unconcerned.

— Where are the chestnuts?

— In my schoolbag, I said innocently.

— Who said you could take them?

— Nobody.

— Put out your hand.

I put out my hand. I thought she was going to give me more chessies but instead of a hard round chessie I felt her lightly slap my hand. It wasn't sore but I understood that this was some kind of punishment. All very formal and precise, not the usual method where your mother would hold you by the arm with one hand and skite the backs of your bare legs with the other, as they frantically tried to outrun her – you half-suspended, half-swinging from her grip.

The worst was the time in the back garden in Sedan Terrace. I was pretending I was going to the toilet, using an appropriate piece of wood to simulate both a functioning penis and that product of the other going-to-the-toilet business where you had to sit down (there was no word for it). That Eileen Cathcart was with me during this performance, and was doing everything I did with her own spectacular piece of wood, seemed to make things worse. Whatever I had done wrong, it was bad. It had something to do with going to the toilet, and girls not going to the toilet the same way as boys, and girls not having a penis. I heard the word 'immodest'. I didn't know what it meant, but I got my legs slapped anyway as I was led back into the house, my perfectly formed wooden penis discarded in the flowerbed and Eileen Cathcart left standing alone still tightly gripping hers. Girls, I tearfully decided even then, must be as tricky as the Catlick/Prodesan thing.

It was one of those long summer mornings of sunburnt arms and legs. I thought I was the bee's knees in my purple tank top and my baggy canvas shorts held up by a red and white snake belt. What with the freshly whitened gutties, I felt colourful and cool in a four-year-old sort of way. There was a bag of crisps in my mother's red string shopping bag and she said that my hair was standing on me.

We wandered about all morning. Into the airy church, around the shining shops and up to the windy graveyard to say a prayer for everybody asleep under the grass. After that we walked round the Ramp, back over the bridge, past the hawthorn trees and up to the hospital to see one of her friends who had just had a baby. I wanted to see the wee baby too, because I had no brothers or sisters of my own. My mother told me that the hospital was the place where you went to get your babies.

— I thought God gave you babies?

— He does, but you have to collect them at the hospital.

I pondered this for a moment, unconvinced.

The maternity ward was like the pet shop – glass cages, fish tanks, funny smells and noises and crinkly little babies asleep in their aquariums, all tubes and plastic pipes. My mother talked some kind of code to her friend and gave her a big bottle of Lucozade. I sat on the edge of the bed and hoped that we could collect a baby too, a little brother for me. After all, this was the place where God left the babies to be collected. We left without one and I sulked a bit. My mother hoked through her shopping bag and soon the bag of crisps had cheered me up again, shaking the last corner crumbs into my scaldie mouth.

I had two goldfish once. My mother bought them for me in the pet shop and I carried them home in a plastic bag full of water. They lived in a bowl in the back hall. One night there was a thunderstorm and next morning one of the goldfish was floating belly-up on the surface. My mother said that it must have been frightened by all the thunder and lightning. The next morning the other one was dead. My mother said that maybe the poor wee thing had died of a broken heart.

Mrs Martin warned the rest of the class not to take anything that didn't belong to them. But I knew that! Never take anything that doesn't belong to you – that was stealing. I knew that. She said that the chestnuts belonged to the nature table and then she looked at me again and smiled.

— The chestnuts belong to the nature table, all right, John?

— They belong to God, I said.

I wasn't being smart but she had to agree.

On the first day we did spellings and it was all easy stuff. CAT and HAT and MAT. We were each given a book about Dick and Dora and their Mum and Dad. Their dad wore a hat and smoked a pipe and went to work with a leather case. I told the teacher that my dad was called Daddy, that he went to work with a lunch box and that he did not smoke a pipe. Dick and Dora had a dog and a cat, and I thought they were very lucky to have room for a dog and a cat and I guessed that they must be English. I had cousins in England and they had dogs and cats and called their mothers and fathers Mum and Dad and they thought that pish-the-beds were fairies. 'Pish-the-bed' was not a nice word. And you were supposed to say door instead of *do-er* and floor instead of *flu-er* and never ask for *tae* the way Babby did.

After school my granny held me by the hood of my anorak and took me across the road. She said there were a lot of bad cubs running about and that they had no manners. She meant the boys who had crossed the road by themselves and were climbing the big tree outside her window. I wanted to join them and climb the tree and jump out of the tree and shout, 'Geronimo!' but she said they were far too rough.

— Did you get slapped? she asked with a smile.

— I did surely.

She was shocked.

— Mother of God! On your first day! God take care of us!

I explained myself and she was horrified.

— You can't take anything not belonging to you – and well you know it. Them chestnuts belonged to the school.

— They belong to God, I said.

I wasn't being smart but, just like Mrs Martin, she had to agree.

What I remember of Primary Two is Sister Margaret and that I liked her. She kept white mice in a tank and we fed them every day. She let us put them on our heads and they crawled everywhere. They had pink feet. The other thing I remember is how much a balaclava made your neck itch. I hated wearing one but nearly all of us in the class were forced into it by our mothers constantly warning us that we might get our deaths. 'Balaclava' – there was a word.

6

If the granny had seen the rough boys in Alphabet City she'd have had a fit. As soon as I rounded that corner I got the message. This was heroin country and the danger was palpable. I realised my mistake and turned like a hare back up towards St Mark's Place and the safe ground of Greenwich Village. This is the other real shock of New York. Yes, it feels like a movie set, but it certainly is not. In fact, it is the very place you have been warned about all your life. Mind yourself. Be careful where you go. Come in out of there, you'll get your death. Don't go near the water, you'll be drowned.

In one uneasy joint I found myself sharing the bar with a genuine real live gang – all of them dressed like Aaron

Neville, all bandanas and leather. I read the code immediately, assumed my full height, tried to walk out like Robert Mitchum but only managed a lame John Wayne. I was waiting for a hand on the shoulder but it never happened and I emerged into the light very grateful that I hadn't got my scaredy-custard head in my hands.

Once safely outside in the bright light, I imagined my heroic warp spasm and the cartoon heap of gang members left in my wake, the barman peering over the top of the counter in disbelief and a frantic cop looking for witnesses. Kojak arriving, slamming the car door, lollipop in his gob and his head tilted with determination to one side.

— Don't be gettin' into any gangs, I was told again and again. There's nothin' only gangs.

And sure enough, gangs were formed from the very first day at school. Small, harmless gangs like the Three Musketeers, crossing swords in the air and shouting:

— All for one and one for all!

And other gangs of cowboys and bandits and soldiers and pirates fighting imaginary battles on the grass. Later, the nastier gangs that kicked and punched and chased one another round the school yard in stampeding hordes – even venturing with courage into the big boys' yard and a more lethal war. I took part, but only as a lookout, preferring even then the solo gig. Better the lone operative taking his own chances than the helpless foot soldier going over the top on the orders of the self-appointed.

In Primary Three there was the Arsenal gang and the Manchester United gang. Two streams neatly divided in their allegiance and coming to blows in the school yard. Mrs McHugh's class all United fans and Sister Ann's all Gunners. It eventually got out of hand and Mrs McHugh suddenly arrived into our class for a whispered conference with Sister Ann. The top of the blackboard was being crawled over by a great blue caterpillar of twenty-six segments, each containing a letter of the alphabet. I read them backwards and forwards to myself as I awaited the inquisition.

— OK, said Sister Ann, I take it that everybody in Mrs McHugh's class has a favourite team and that team is Manchester United?

I booed quietly and a few others backed me up.

— Be quiet, she snapped. And I understand that everybody in this class supports Arsenal.

I cheered (under my breath).

Sister Ann said that all the fighting would have to stop, and then she smiled.

— Put up your hand if you support Arsenal.

Everybody put up their hand except for one boy. He thought he would get into trouble and just kept his head down and sulked. I never forgot his spineless treachery and was secretly pleased when he left the school shortly afterwards. I was proud that the rest of us had stood up for what we believed in, just like Blessed Oliver Plunkett or Muhammad Ali.

Over the next few years the Arsenal fans deserted for Leeds United or Liverpool and only a few of us were left, like the eleven apostles hiding in the room, waiting for glorious news and hoping against hope.

After those fractures the school yard became considerably nastier. Smart arses, slags and bullies developed their skills and began to exercise their cruelty on the weak. I was never particularly picked on in school because I was tall and I wasn't fat. Slagged, yes, but never actually bullied in the real sense of the word. People shouting 'big ears' or

singing, 'John Kelly broke his belly sliding down a lumpa
jelly' was about the height of it. Hearing that my father had
been on the receiving end of the same singsong rhyme (and
probably my grandfather too) turned the slag into an
occasion of pride and became another of the connections I
was anxious for some reason to make.

Dumbo the Flying Elephant really did hurt and being
told that I should be happy that was the way God made
me didn't ease the pain. But I could take it reasonably well
(some of the time) and rarely ever lost the head. Just as
well, because I was never a scrapper. I always thought far
too deeply and usually foresaw the inevitable terrible
consequences. Teachers would be involved, parents would
be involved, and a whole ritual of disapproval would
follow. Fear of getting in trouble was my yellow streak and
too much sense was my failing.

Every scrap, even those not preorganised, began with
two boys dunting each other.

— Piss off!
— Naw!
— Go on, piss off!
— Who's gonna make me?
— I'll make you!
— You and whose army?
— I'll bust ye so I will!

And a crowd would gather and smell blood and all the
time these idiotic dunts and half-shoulder charges. The
circle of slavering spectators would begin to chant for their
man – always for the same man. It didn't matter who was
your friend and who wasn't. Certain people commanded
support in all circumstances.

— Come on, Pa-dee! Come on, Pa-dee!

Eventually, often against the will of both participants,

there followed a wild embrace of hair pulling, ear grabbing and tears, and then the sudden appearance of an outraged nun, who would devote the whole afternoon to the inquisition and punishment of our two heroes, now reduced to quivering cowards terrified of the note home.

I confess that I often bitterly regret my own precocious sense. I wish now that I'd acted my age and thumped a few people without grown-up regard to the consequences and not cared a hoot what my mother would say. It would have made certain childhood episodes much easier to have survived and in moments of heroic fantasy I am sometimes back in that playground, coming off the ropes like Ali and punching various hateful bastards up and down the yard. No kicking or gouging, mind you, all good clean stuff – jabs, uppercuts and huge sweeping hooks that lift these little shites off their feet and leave them in crumpled, miserable, tangled heaps.

This strain of regrettable good sense was matched by yet another unfortunate sort of innocence it took a long time to shake off.

— What's a count? I once asked my mother and my granny and my Aunty Peggy after school.

— A what?

— A big boy at school called me a count and a bullock.

There was no immediate response but my father must have been consulted and soon the response came back.

— Your daddy says those are not nice words.

I never used a bad word until I was about eight and got free with 'flip' and 'bloomin', and even then not in front of my mother and father. Flip was bad, frig was worse, feck was next and then the other word that seemed, with relevant modifications, to serve as noun, verb and adjective.

— Do you hear that oul' bad talk, the granny would complain. All that effin' and blindin' – the whole word!

All this linguistic censorship got to me early and resulted in the first time I was actually lost for words. Primary Three. Break time. Football match. The teams had been picked and were already facing each other when myself and Sam Ferguson arrived looking a game. The captain had to pick whoever he wanted for his team and he was one of my best friends. I was certain he would pick me. He didn't.

Overcome with rage and betrayal, I stared at him full of venom, searching for the right term of abuse.

— You – you – you –

In hindsight the word I needed is obvious enough, but in those days that wasn't an option. I didn't say bad words. I didn't lift my foot to anyone. I didn't throw stones in case I put somebody's eye out. I groped around for an appropriate word that wasn't a bad word and suddenly out came my best shot.

— You – you – you – codger!

I have no idea where I got that word from – some comic no doubt – but I remember saying it. I could take you to the very spot. I felt an immediate burning foolishness and the cascades of laughter and confusion all around me.

— What did he call him?

— A codger or something – I dunno –

— A what?

Another moment I would like a second go at and be a hero not just in my own head.

Wembley Stadium. London. England. 1971. Arsenal FC have just won the League and Cup double, beating Liverpool FC by two goals to one after extra time. The winning goal by a long-haired twenty-year-old with sideburns is being played and replayed. Slow motion action replay. His name is Charlie George and he is lying on his back on the Wembley turf. A quare-lookin' sketch, my father said. The commentator is screaming:

— The fans are on the pitch! And even Mr Burtenshaw has collapsed.

In Enniskillen, County Fermanagh, Northern Ireland, 1971, I am a six-year-old with a short back and sides. I am skinny but tall for my age, all elbows, knees and freckles, and I have scored the winning goal at Wembley. Slow motion action replay and I am lying on my own back on my own tarmac.

The back windows of our house look out onto a sloping tarmacadamed car park with three garages full of junk and cars and boats and engines and a huge dead pike. Here we played and dreamt football until it was too dark to see your finger. And here we dreamt as we played football, determined to forego meals, bedtime, and going to the bogs. At one end, Artie Stephenson's fence. At the other, the square iron door of Dicksons' garage. Each had its own special sound to herald a goal: the planks of Artie's fence would thud and rattle and Dicksons' garage door would crash and dent – both magnificent and glorious noises.

Football in a car park surrounded by grandstands of kitchens and bedrooms meant, of course, that there was bound to be the odd disaster. All it took was a reckless volley or a premeditated toe-pointer and the breaking of a window was somehow a *very* serious offence. Honour demanded that Rivelino's father had to pay for the damage and often personally install its replacement. It was the worst thing you could do to your parents. It was not some ordinary misdemeanour that could be covered up. This brought with it all the full palaver of the scrap – parents, inquisition and maybe even the police (the pull-ees). It didn't matter a continental damn that the damage had been done by a René van de Kerkhof forty-yarder or a peach of a free kick by Gunter Netzer of Borussia Mönchengladbach that had us all quivering in our gutties and cupping our hands over our groins. It made no odds either that for one brief moment a boy had kicked beyond himself, kicked through into something else, and that the confirmation of that breakthrough was the terrific sound of breaking glass and a gaping, stunned silence on the Stretford End. It made no odds.

Rescuing the ball from gardens and flowerbeds was also a hazard. Old Mr Cassidy regularly captured a prized Wembley football and held it hostage in his kitchen. We would gaze helplessly, like cattle looking over a gate, as he set the ball on his kitchen table and rummaged through drawers for his sharpest and most vicious knife. Some of us would spit lazily through our teeth and others would rehearse their vaguely threatening knowledge of the laws of trespass and theft. The more spirited invoked the possibility of brotherly intervention, older, ferocious and violent avengers who would put old Mr Cassidy in his box. Bust him!

But then all bravado would evaporate as he emerged from his kitchen with the ball wedged under his oxter and him wielding a terrifying-looking carving knife. It was always a horrible moment when he threatened to murder our football.

— Nobody move or the ball gets it!

And then there were girls and dogs. Most of the local dogs were treated almost as equals. They turned out for most of our matches and several were accomplished players. Bonzo

Hynes belonged to Rosie Hynes, who had a grotto in her garden and made ice lollies. Bonzo was a gangly and slightly daft dog who always caused havoc in the six-yard area. Caesar Curry belonged to Stevie Curry and was a large, black, regal Labradorish dog, a solid player in the Franz Beckenbauer mould who could put his paw on the ball and hold up the entire game, just like the Kaiser himself. Rags McGubbin belonged to Bob, who drove a Spitfire, and Rags was a terrier, extremely good in the air but also rather over-zealous, bad-tempered and cynical, not averse to biting the legs of dribbling wingers. Big Norman Hunter at Elland Road had nothing on Rags McGubbin. We didn't really mind dogs playing, although they usually played for both sides at once and rarely lasted the ninety minutes.

The real problem was the girls. We hated them and they hated us. Knowing that we considered them useless, they adopted all manner of disruptive tactics. Sit-down protests or simply leaning against Artie Stephenson's fence or Dicksons' garage, defiantly chewing their penny chews and admiring the chipped red varnish on their toes.

— Will yous cutties get off the pitch!

— Naw, it's a free country!

— Get out of the goals, yous stupid bitches!

— Yous don't own the place!

— Frig off!

— If you hit me with that ball –

Then a stand-off. All of the boys and all of the dogs staring out all of the dirty-faced girls in their dirty white socks, slapping about in their mothers' dirty white stilettos and singing:

Georgie Best, superstar,
Wears frilly knickers and he wears a bra.

Eventually some one of us, one of the madder ones, would start lobbing the ball at them. They would stand their ground and the chips and lobs would then become sidefoot taps that got harder and harder until one of the girls would be hurt and in tears. The others would get deeply offended and begin to impersonate their mothers, getting all litigious, moralistic and uglier by the minute. And then the breakdown and the determined march into the house and the screamed threats.

— Yous are in for it now! My father's in the UDR and he has a gun in the house. He'll bloody well put manners on yous!

It wasn't easy being Charlie George in Northern Ireland in the early seventies and things were getting trickier by the day.

We were glory hunters and we understood perfectly well what was superhuman about a forty-yarder or going past three defenders and chipping the keeper. When we scored we punched the air with that aggressive little gesture of Stuart Pearson's, or held one arm aloft like Sniffer Clarke, or better still – as long as there were no Prodesans around – we would do a Jairzinho. Just like the great Brazilian, we would fall to our knees, raise our faces to heaven and bless ourselves. We understood even then that such moments of skill were manifestations of something supernatural called *a gift* – what commentators called *magic*.

There was nothing like scoring. It was the greatest and most important thing a young boy could do. To connect cleanly with a full volley, right on the instep, and the ball would thud and ring and thump against Artie Stephenson's fence or smash against Dicksons' garage door.

— Kelly! One–nil!

And we had another very strange ability – we could commentate on our own matches as we played them.

— Best – past one – past two – still Best – magic stuff from Best – past three – past four – oh, he nutmegs McCalliog – this is sheer genius – still Best – just the keeper to beat – he chips the keeper – oh my word! can you believe it – Best – six–nil!

These commentaries were always in impeccable English accents. We got our football from English television and that's the way we heard it. It wasn't that football was actually played in England – I had only a vague idea of where England was – it was simply that football was played on the television and that football and footballers existed in some parallel universe. Highbury was where Arsenal played and it had Marble Halls.

Another way into this world was through a magazine called *Shoot!* I could hardly wait to collect the copy my granny had put on order for me – all part of the delight of a Friday and no school for two days. Such excitement when it featured a full-colour centre-spread team photograph of Arsenal. Suddenly all these new faces and names, the new signings and reserves to add to my store of heroes. Peter Marinello – the new George Best. Anyone who read *Shoot!* knew everything about his club, from the number of times it had won the FA Cup to the name of the groundsman's dog.

'Focus On' was a feature where a player was asked a series of personal questions. Who in the whole world would you most like to meet? Favourite food? Biggest drag in football? They all wanted to meet either Muhammad Ali or Steve McQueen. Peter Osgood wanted to meet Claudia Cardinale, whoever she was – sounded religious to me. Joe Corrigan, the keeper at Maine Road, wanted to meet the

pope. He must have been a Catlick. Favourite food was
always scampi.

'You are the Ref' was a section of the magazine compiled
by Stan Lover and it aimed to teach the rules of the game.
A cartoon strip scenario presented a problem and you were
put in the role of the referee. A keeper taking too many
steps. An incorrectly taken throw. Facts, information,
statistics, away strips, baloney. There was a time in my
childhood where I came alarmingly close to genius.

We did have soccer of our own but that didn't count. As
far as we were concerned, it was just a boring postscript on
a Saturday evening. Time for the tea. After the weird ritual
of the teleprinter and the solemn incantations of James
Alexander-Gordon, our own local results would crash onto
the screen from a cheap-looking studio in Belfast.
Crusaders, Distillery, Glentoran, Linfield, Cliftonville – a
series of no-score draws played out on grey days by
scrappy semi-professionals somewhere in and around
Belfast. Instead of Highbury, Stamford Bridge, White Hart
Lane, Selhurst Park and Old Trafford, the Irish League had
the Oval, Seaview, Windsor, and the home of Cliftonville,
almost unbelievably called Solitude. Saturday suddenly
suspended and put on hold until *Dr Who* and *The
Generation Game*.

What we were doing with such conviction and glory in
that sloping car park was our Fermanagh version of
barefoot Brazilians on the beach at Rio. Pelé juggling with a
pineapple. And we were just as good as any of those
Brazilians – none of them would try a bicycle kick on
tarmac! None of their goalkeepers would dive on concrete
like Ernie McVitty. The banana shot. The sliding tackle.
The scissor kick.

And then one afternoon Brother Barney finally lost the

rag and pulled us in off the pitch.

— No more PE! Ye're all useless!

He had been watching our effort at a soccer match on an uphill all-weather pitch. An awkward swarm of forty boys all chasing the ball and no obvious skill on display. It was a sorry spectacle right enough, and Brother Barney had reached the end of his Presentation Brother tether. Like Jesus in the temple, he scattered us in all directions and ordered us back to class.

We all liked Brother Barney. He had bushy eyebrows and he called Donald Duck Dónal Duck. He was always very good to us and one time we managed, from all those slobbery heaps of frogspawn, to rear a frog. First the tapioca, then the growing eye, then the million shapeless fish. After that the big-head tadpoles eating each other and charging the sides of the tank – mad, evil, miniature monsters with teeth. And then there was just the one left with sprouting legs and a full stomach. We got nips of meat from the dinner hall and fed our weird creation every day until suddenly he was a magical wee frog to be carried like Moses to the rushes.

All that easy-going happiness seemed to be over now as Brother Barney waited for us all to take our seats. Why had he ordered us back to class? What had happened? What was he going to do? Everything was nervously out of kilter as he turned to the blackboard and began to draw strange diagrams in chalk.

— This, he began with great passion, is the way to play soccer football. Leeds United. Johnny Giles. Triangles. You don't run about like a crowd of sheep after the ball. Triangles. One man here.

He butted the chalk against the board with a crack.

— Another man here!

Another crack.

— Another man here! Johnny Giles!

Another crack and the chalk broke. We didn't laugh – this was far too strange a lesson.

— Triangles! Triangles! Triangles!

He gave us no homework that night. No spellings and no sums. When the granny asked me what I had learnt that day I told her that I had learnt tactics. It must have sounded impressive – like ethics or physics – and she seemed satisfied. If she had known it was football she'd have lamented:

— Ah, football! Nothin' only football!

7

The chill factor was getting the better of me. As Tom Waits would sing, it was colder than a well-digger's ass. I had been breaking all the rules about wet hair and damp boots and was suffering from a ferocious dose of the cold. In the drugstore on Lexington I could imagine my mother's voice.

— Don't go out in them wet shoes. Dry your hair. You'll get your death. There's nothing worse than a wettin'.

I sniffily gathered lozenges, powders and potions and back in the hotel room, like someone altogether crazy, I opened my own pharmaceutical store and took to drying my boots with a hairdryer. A cold or a flu at once turns me into a child – a common symptom of illness among men. I become immediately helpless, miserable and frustrated. I want to lie there like a walrus breathing through my mouth and be handed steaming mugs of hot lemon juice. Better still, I feel I deserve a day off school.

— Where's Kelly this morning?

— He's got the flu, Master.

— He has, my eye, says the Master.

— He has, I saw him, Master. He was all snatters!

— That's enough, McManus. And where's Maguire today? I suppose he has this contagion as well.

— He has the jandies, Master.

— Are you a doctor, McManus?

— No, Master. But he has the jandies, so he has.

— The word is 'jaundice', McManus.

— He's all yella, Master.

— Anybody else sick?

McKernan puts up his hand.

— I have the measles, Master, and I used to have the chicken pox. And the mumps too. And my granny had a bad back one time but it was cured at Lourdes.

— That's quite enough, McKernan.

Peggy had been to Lourdes, too, but she didn't get better and her hands were still different. Even so, she said the woman in the ward beside her had been cured and there had been great excitement. She prayed on like a saint in a cell. Prayed for everybody, especially me. I heard somewhere that suffering was a blessing from God.

All the time religion. The answers were there for all to learn by rote in an orange-coloured book called the Catechism. Who is God? What is my soul? What is a sacrament? Why is there suffering in the world? I forget all those answers now except perhaps for one, that a sacrament is an outward sign of inward grace, and I only remember it because it was all part of that intensive religious instruction around the time of First Confession and First Communion.

Everything was simple then. And what could be simpler or more ingenious than a little book with drawings which not only gave me the answers, it gave me the questions as well?

Up until this point, religion had amounted to prayers and mantras and wonderful stories from the Bible. We loved those stories – Moses and the Pharaoh's army, the Good Samaritan, the Nativity. And the boy in the class who drew a picture of the Flight into Egypt – a jumbo jet high over the Pyramids and the three smiling faces of Jesus, Mary and Joseph at the window. In the cockpit the grinning stick figure of Pontius the Pilot.

Such stories! As good as Jason and the Argonauts, the Ulster Cycle or the King with the Ass's Ears. These stories were periodically read and we could simply sit and listen – better than sums or comprehension and not much scope for ritual slapping and dusters over the head. Best of all was the Crucifixion and the drama that surrounded that one. We lapped up every painful detail and our minds raced in fear and fascination. The Agony in the Garden, the Judas kiss, Peter lopping off that fella's ear, the trial.

— It is you who say it.

Baldy Telly Savalas, the cock crowing three times, the scourging, the crown of thorns, the nails, the blood and on and on and on it went. The Passion rationed out over days. No wonder we were transfixed in horror and awe and something like disbelief.

But now with First Confession and First Communion, a new and, on the face of it, less childish approach to religion

had to be taken. It was no longer enough just to draw and
paint our macabre Crucifixions, the three writhing figures
and the centurion (John Wayne) saying, 'Truly this man
was the son of Gaad.'

At seven we had allegedly reached the age of reason and
my father bought me a watch. I wanted one with a black
face, a Sekonda, and I was extra pleased that it was
Russian and that it glowed in the dark. I wandered about
with one sleeve rolled up asking everyone to ask me the
time.

We were now supposed to know the difference
between good and bad. And so all of us were, for a
while, preoccupied with realising, unearthing, uncovering
and, in some cases, inventing our own virtually nonexistent sins. This was called 'examining your conscience'
and it was a very difficult procedure which involved
working your way through the Ten Commandments and
devising some cunning way in which you could claim to
have broken them (even if you hadn't). This was never
easy. After all, many of the Commandments could be
discarded immediately, oxen, wives and murder having
little bearing on our young lives. Even so, we never let
that stop us in our endless search for confessable sin. I
know of one piece of penitential creativity where a young
sinner calmly admitted to murdering his wee brother. The
priest apparently laughed and told him not to tell lies in
the confession box. The freckled murderer was not
amused.

— Wouldn't friggin' believe me, the bastard.

The answer, I soon realised, was not to exaggerate. Try
to come up with sins that were believable – stealing apples,
kicking your brother or sister (I didn't have either), saying
bad words (codger) and plenty of adultery.

— And who did you commit adultery with, if you don't mind me asking?

— Loads of people, Father, loads of people.

There were two types of sin – venial and mortal. Venial was a small sin and mortal was a big sin. If you died with a venial sin on your soul you would go to purgatory, which was a kind of holding centre. If you died with a mortal sin on your soul you would go straight to hell. Fire. Devils with horns and red-hot pokers. Die with no sins on your soul and you would go straight to heaven and sit on a cloud with the angels and see God.

Your soul was like your heart although it wasn't really there at all. Whenever you committed a sin a black spot appeared on it, and the more you sinned the blacker it got and finally it rotted like a bad potato. When you died it was your soul that went to heaven, but it had to be spotless. The only way to guarantee this was to die with no sins on your soul and the best bet was to get run over by a lorry or struck by lightning the second you came out of the confession box. I often pondered this and wondered what would happen if you stepped out into the aisle all pure and forgiven and you suddenly saw a juggernaut coming straight at you and you said to yourself, Oh fuck, there's some bastard driving a lorry straight at me! Would that be bad enough to send you to purgatory? Surely a bit unfair to go to hell under the circumstances? And there was never any answer to that one in the Catechism. Never.

The more I thought about it the more complicated and unconvincing it all got. It didn't seem to matter which way you turned, sin and damnation were waiting, and the big cover-all clause was the small print from Genesis about original sin, a sin which was on your white potato soul even though you had not committed it yourself. It was

Adam and Eve's fault, and they were our first parents. They had committed a sin (nyuckin' an apple) and we were stuck with it. The only way to get rid of this black mark was to be baptised and anybody could do a baptism in an emergency. You could even use water out of a puddle if you were stuck. And what if you were run over by a lorry before you were baptised? You went to limbo. And what and where was limbo? I asked more than enough times and never got a proper answer. (Now they tell me it has been shut down, theologically speaking, and possibly was never open in the first place.)

There was a solemn and very nervous rehearsal for First Communion. Sister Ann pretended to be the priest and said, 'Body of Christ' and we said, 'Amen', and stuck out our tongues and she touched our tongues with the tip of her blue Biro. We wondered what the bread would taste like and we were warned that it might get stuck to the roofs of our mouths and that we were to swallow it reverently and were not to chew it. Babby said that I was not to let it touch my teeth at all.

On the day itself, everything ran smoothly. The bread tasted like cardboard and kind of dissolved, and I thought I could smell the wine from the priest's fingers. The boys were on one side in their short trousers and their ties with the elastic under the collar and the girls were on the other, like little brides with their white veils and handbags. After Communion we all waited expectantly for something to happen, scrutinising each other's tightly closed lips and gazing serenely at the Transfiguration high above the altar. Nothing happened and the fearless giggled.

Afterwards we were given money by relations and we posed for a class photograph. Hands joined just like the priest's, like a holy bug-eyed football team transforming

into gargoyles and demons before your very eyes.
— How much money did *you* get?

The bronze door of St Patrick's on Fifth Avenue was as irresistible as any door into any darkness. Once inside, I was surrounded by candles and the sight of elderly women in side aisles whispering frantically to themselves and looking like they'd been there all their lives. I thought once more of whoever it was belonging to me who lived on Fifth Avenue and imagined their first Sunday in New York when Fifth Avenue didn't extend beyond Forty-second Street. I thought of them jerkily genuflecting and kneeling down, the men with one knee on their caps, the women with their shawls, and praying for the people at home, lighting candles and looking at the ceiling for a sign. Maybe singing in best guttural Fermanagh:

We will be true to thee till death,
We will be true to thee till death.

I wondered too about the Mrs Eugene Kelly who donated 200,000 dollars to help build Dagger John's St Patrick's in the first place. She must have been made of money. And here's one – they say that Orangemen rioted in Greenwich Village in 1824. Would you credit that?

I wandered over to P.J. Clarke's to play Artie Shaw and Billie Holiday on the glowing altar of a jukebox and to wait for some friends. Round the corner was Michael's. Woody was in town and he would probably show tonight. We settled in Clarke's and I talked about Ray Milland and Kipperlugs, kicking his own dog up the Cornagrade Road. Thanks to the blizzard of '96, Rudi Giuliani and Batman, there was just us – and the man outside screaming.

— I got AIDS, man! It's cold, man! It's real cold, man! No answer to that one either.

EXTERIOR/INTERIOR — P.J. CLARKE'S — NIGHT

[*The camera shows snowdrift in front of door and moves inside past drinkers in quiet, almost empty, bar to Kelly and friends with their backs to the jukebox. Michael Collins is on the wall. The barman looks up over his glasses now and again. Kelly and his friends are talking about music and anxiously looking out the window at heavy snow. Kelly is particularly worried and the camera moves in close on his face. He has a red, runny nose.*]

KELLY Do you think he'll show tonight? They're expecting him. He's in town all right.

BARMAN He might – I dunno. He plays the first set so you can make it back in here later. You can tell me all about it. Another late night, eh kid?

KELLY Aye, your arse! Early night tonight. If I don't get at least sixteen hours, I'm a basket case.

SMALL PASSING CHILD That's a good 'un, fucksake!

CUT TO EXTERIOR/INTERIOR — WOODY'S ROOM — NIGHT

[*Camera shows Woody's glasses close up at windowpane and pulls back to reveal him full length and agitated. He turns and the camera moves in through the blur of snowflakes to a warm apartment. Woody packs his clarinet and keeps looking out the window at heavy snow.*]

WOODY Uugh! It's terrible. But I got this ... uh [*clears his throat*] gig to do. I might ... uh [*clears his throat*] get my death. And Kelly's going to be there. Jeez, I'm so tense. [*Clears his throat*] I enjoy his poems. Particularly the early funny ones.

FADE TO BLACK — END CREDITS

As a conscious act of industry, notes were scribbled on tissues and calling cards. Sitting in P.J. Clarke's would not get a book written, but then much thinking, ruminating and cogitating still had to be done. And so, scraps of paper and sparked-off memories kept my conscience relatively clear, and we sat on high stools talking music. The company was good. The scraps piled up. One near-illegible scribble on a receipt read simply: FEIS. SINGING. RECORDER.

In Primary Five the school choir was suddenly introduced to the Irish language when a rousing song was written phonetically on the blackboard.

Fake taw shin na clann na hayran
Chocked le keyle inyou anshaw.

And we sang like little sweet robots without a baldy's notion what we were singing. And when we sang the song at the *feis* we won a cup and beat the girls and that was all that mattered. I had a reasonable voice and sang anonymously happy in the tiered ranks but refused with great conviction to ever sing solo. There was something unacceptable about it. I think I was put off even then by the parents of the many who did. They would turn up with their awful offspring and parade them around like poodles at a dog show. It seemed that they lived, in some unnaturally vicarious way, through them. Enter as many competitions as possible, arrange for extra tuition so they would sing with fake enthusiasm, and then triumphantly comb their overwashed hair before lining them up victorious in front of the cameras of the *Fermanagh Herald* and the *Impartial Reporter*.

I only went solo twice. Once in Omagh where nobody knew me and once when I took the head-staggers in Ederney. I got a silver and a bronze for singing 'Slán le Corcaigh' and I remember my parents were slightly amazed. I was a bit surprised myself.

Competitions were often surreal events. In his book *Last Night's Fun* Ciaran Carson tells a story about two adjudicators who were as full as forty badgers, performed a duet themselves, and awarded *everyone* a medal. There's a strong chance that I was one of those too-generously treated chanters. Best to let the hare sit, all the same. The medal is not going back now – drunk adjudicators or not.

Apart from those particular freakish solo incidents, all singing was done amongst the sheltering harmonies of my soprano classmates. I half-learnt the recorder too, but couldn't care less about crotchets and quavers and minims. I could play it but had no interest in *learning* it. 'Clair de Lune', I think, was my dull, passionless party piece, but the whole point of the recorder was to progress to the clarinet or the flute (James Galway was the in thing) and that meant music lessons after school. Again I recoiled in disgust. My parents weren't the type to dispatch me to piano lessons or trumpet lessons or Irish dancing lessons or any other lesson, for that matter, that I didn't want to go to. For this sober generosity I was, and still am, grateful. And why would I have wanted to go, anyway? Wasting my time playing scales and stupid tunes when I could be out kicking football.

These were my little rebellions. Music lessons and whatever else were all demands that I submit to yet more authority and so surrender parts of my life. I wanted to remain free from this, to wander off collecting fossils and stones, to fish for roach and perch and bream. That was much more important. When the priest came looking for new altar boys I said no, and no questions were asked.

I wish now that I *had* learnt the piano, but back then there seemed no sense to it. I hadn't yet heard Duke Ellington or Art Tatum or Doctor John or Jerry Lee Lewis. I certainly wish now that I had learnt the clarinet or the saxophone, but back then I had never heard of Sidney Bechet or John Coltrane or Sonny Rollins. If only some educator had led me towards a Blue Note record instead of giving me endless spellings and sums, a boogie-woogie instead of 'Twinkle, Twinkle, Little Star'.

We took our seats in Michael's and ordered Cajun chicken and, sure enough, Woody arrived wearing an army jacket and cords. He was carrying his clarinet case and he looked exactly like Woody Allen – sad-eyed, hunched, nervy and shy. I remembered a scene in *Hannah and Her Sisters* when, desperate to uncover some meaning in life, he is telling a Hare Krishna in Central Park how he had tried to be a Catlick for a week. He said he couldn't get into it because it was die now, pay later. If only I'd had a line like that as I picked at the clouded plastic stuck to the classroom window. There would be no answer to that one in the book full of answers to its very own questions.

8

Cab downtown to Greenwich Village, the back seat swimming in melted snow. I was to meet Pete Hamill at Ireland House, part of an academic oasis off Washington Square with its sentries of hissing dope-sellers. Pete was doing a television interview about his new collection of journalism, *Piece Work*, and Ireland House was silent with crew, cables and lights.

All the talk was of ceasefires, Clinton, Mitchell, talks, historic opportunity and deepening doubt. No escape seems possible (even if desired) from this place called Northern Ireland, the broad-minded cursing the narrow-minded and sighing in despair.

Interview under way, I padded about upstairs, where an

old Currier and Ives print displayed a moustachioed man in ankle boots and green trousers with white trims: JOHN ENNIS. THE CELEBRATED PEDESTRIAN. IRELAND. Close reading revealed that he was second in the International Pedestrian Six Days' Contest with O'Leary, Powell and Harrington for the Astley Champion Belt at Gilmore's Garden, New York, 10–15 March 1879. The distance covered was 475 miles and 300 yards. Took him five days, twenty-one hours, three minutes and, quite remarkably, forty-nine seconds.

In the office the talk was of Brodsky, Walcott and Heaney.

— What are *you* writin' these days? Pete asked.

I laughed at the turn the conversation would now have to take. I explained my lesser purpose.

— How's it going?

— Slowly, I confessed.

— Are you using a computer?

— Not at the minute, I said, thinking of the hotel room littered with pages and scraps of menus and coasters and corners of newspapers.

— Try longhand, suggested Pete, on a yellow pad.

We talked about articles he had written in *Esquire*, the *Village Voice* and *New York*, gathered together in his book under the title *The Lawless Decades*. They concerned what Pete described as 'the American slide into urban barbarism'. How in eighties New York there could be twenty-five murders in a single weekend. Pete loves his city. Poverty, drugs and endless murder has made him 'an American liberal who has come to distrust all dogma, including liberal dogma'. The sorry sight of his own society breaks his own decent heart. He writes about how the grand ideal of *e pluribus unum* is being swept away by 'a poisonous flood tide of negation, sectarianism, self-pity, confrontation, vulgarity and flat-out, old-fashioned hatred'. He describes politics as 'an ice-jam of accusation and obstruction', and he laments that society's vulgarians are being rewarded for their cynicism and that society's good men are 'fleeing to tend private gardens'.

That afternoon I tackled the place called Northern Ireland longhand on a yellow pad.

Jim Skelly's yarn. Jim was Head of Religion at the BBC in Belfast and he was taking the Head of Religion from London (an Anglican clergyman, now a bishop) on a tour of Belfast. The drama began when, despite the Head of Religion's unshakable faith in Jim, their car was hijacked on the outskirts of the west of the city. Guns were waved, the car sped off, and Jim and his charge were left standing on a shiny road in the dark.

— What do we do now? enquired the Head of Religion politely.

— Walk, advised Jim.

They reached a house on the very edge of west Belfast and Jim knocked the door.

— Hello, I'm sorry to bother you so late. I'm Father Jim Skelly –

The reply from within was swift.

— Fuck off!

Jim and the Head of Religion walked on and finally gained access to a house. The owner was gracious and produced drinks and called the police. The police arrived. The army arrived. Soon the Head of Religion, a senior policeman and an army major were supping yellow whiskey.

The man of the house then said he would enquire about the car. A call was made, whispered words were exchanged, and then the following announcement was made to the unlikely gathering.

— It's OK, said the man of the house. I know where you can find your car. It wasn't *the boys* – it was the hoods.

Police and army departed and as the Head of Religion from London drank up, he smacked his lips and remarked quietly:

— What a fascinating society you live in.

Throughout the primary school years of sandpits and spelling tests and multiplication tables and catechism and slaps, all sorts of things were happening. This, after all, was Northern Ireland in the seventies, although I wasn't aware of very much of it other than perhaps picking up on feelings of despair and often hearing the word 'terrible' as the wireless talked about 'tit for tat'. Tit for tat was something you heard every morning as you ate your porridge and Veda. It sounded rude because I thought tit was a bad word, although farmers always said it and talked about cows' tits, and also, if anybody told on you they were telltale tits:

Telltale tit
Your mammy can't knit
Your granny's gonna buy you a dummy tit.

I examined my upside-down reflection in the spoon and wondered about this awful place Belfast, where people got killed, and I was glad I lived safe in Enniskillen.

— They've gone clean mad, Babby said.

Enniskillen had not yet become a headline. It was the border garrison town to which dragoons sang fare thee well and where Saint Patrick's mother kept a shebeen house. Skintown. Picturesque and waterlogged Island of

Ceithle in the heart of the County Fermanagh for muscle
and bone. Market town in a damp border county that the
blow-ins were starting to call the Lakeland.

The fair of Enniskillen is the greatest fair of all.
The girls they are the prettiest
And the boys are straight and tall.

I once asked Josef Locke to sign a copy of his greatest
hits for me and he wrote, 'Good luck to the Skins', and
raved about his days in Enniskillen. He had been a
policeman – a sergeant – and he talked of how he had led
the police on a church parade on Sunday mornings, up
Queen Street and left into Darling Street, where the
Methodists peeled off into the pillared Methodist church.
Then, at the top of Hall's Lane, the Church of Ireland
contingent turned left into St Macartan's and the Catholics
turned right into St Michael's. Joe turned right, ascended
the stone spiral staircase to the gallery, and sang his lungs
out in full uniform. Changed times.

But just how innocent is *my* memory? My experience is
certainly not that of someone from Belfast or Derry.
Enniskillen was a relatively quiet town but, even so, things
certainly happened, astonishing events in any child's life.
Deaths, shootings, bombs that shook the houses, huge
rumbling, thundering explosions, the post-bang silence
and the guesswork.

— Sounds like the barracks.

— Sounded more like up the town.

The seventies. Parkas and flares. Parallels and careless
haircuts. Mysterious graffiti – Éire Nua, Stickies, Provos,
1690, No Surrender, and Fuck the Pope. Military. Biscuit
tins. Army men. Bomb disposal. Bugs Bunny. Nudie
women Sellotaped to the door. Creamery cans. Controlled

explosions. Will all keyholders return to their premises. Scottish regiments. Tar and feather.

There were shouting matches every night on television. David Dunseith in the middle and my father practising his drawing. Quick sketches from the screen – Brian Faulkner, Bernadette Devlin, Edward Heath, Paddy Devlin, John Hume, Ian Paisley, Willie Whitelaw – the names and the times are all confused now in my head – but it's a *feeling* I remember. That something awful was happening, and it was going to get worse.

And my first late night. I had woken up sick on a hot and sticky pillow and had staggered bewildered down the stairs, my pyjamas stained with vomit. It was eleven o'clock at night. The light was still on. My parents were still up. The television was on and Paisley was shouting something about the spider saying come into the parlour, and I forgot my sickness because this was a late, late night and it was like another world, almost another dimension, a parallel universe on the other side of the mirror. I gazed around the room, expecting the vases on the mantelpiece to have assumed another shape and the clock to be whirring backwards and forwards. Paisley waved his fist and I stared in wonder at the fireplace as my mother gently washed the boke from my cheek.

— There you are now, you're as right as rain.

What else of Enniskillen in the seventies? Any other manifestations of the Troubles, as they were called, were so regular that we passed no remarks. Endless helicopters with dull, thick rotors and huge wheels, inches over chimney pots and aerials, and then the race to the back window to see them land. And all the time shooting. Volley after volley from the barracks. Sandbags. Barbed wire. Rookies. Elections. Posters. Canvassers. Turnouts.

Fermanagh and South Tyrone. Recounts. Vote early and
vote often.

— Who are you voting for?

— I can't vote. I'm only nine.

— Are you voting for Harry West?

— It's none of your business.

— You'll be voting for Frank Maguire. I know you will.
I'm voting for Harry West, so I am.

— Sure you can't vote either. You're only eight – you
stupid bugger!

For all that was going on in the place called Northern
Ireland, Enniskillen remained for the most part a decent
place. Not that oul' daycency bullshite but the genuine
thing. Extremists were eccentrics, and by and large people
co-existed with great skill, diplomacy and manners.
Methods were developed, and perhaps sociologists and
long-winded academics are the only ones with the jargon
to best describe the give-and-take that went on in daily life.
In and out of each other's houses. First to offer sympathy.
First with the spark plugs. First with the Christmas card
and first with a dependable neighbourly loyalty that
always worked both ways. I can think of a thousand
examples that would confound the biggest bigot and the
sickest cynic. The huge feeds of vinegared chips in what
some might think the most unlikely houses and no remarks
passed when half our number wouldn't say hello to the
other half on the Twelfth. It was all seen as fair enough and
a bit funny.

I can only wonder what was made of *our* bizarre rituals?
I hope to God they were a source of amusement and light-
hearted conversation in the kitchen. Certainly they were
further occasions of touching diplomacy and gesture. I
remember Mrs Quinn politely remarking that it was, she

believed, St Mary's Day, when I went to see her after Mass on the Feast of the Immaculate Conception, a holy day of obligation and a day off school. She had heard something about it on Athlone and said she was sure I had been at church that morning and she gave me 10p. On top of that, she had the wisdom and grace not to ask me what any of it meant. Good job, too. She'd have got a quare and inaccurate answer.

The fact that I can remember a few breakdowns in our tolerant *modus vivendi* makes me feel confident that my memory is reasonable. One such occasion of a virus in the system was when somebody's cousin arrived like a pitbull from Scotland.

— Don't play with them, they're Catholics, he roared.

Everyone was embarrassed in a confused, childish way and I remembered Nigel Johnston and got angry. There was something deeply stupid about whatever this was and it ruined a good match, with the score standing at 56–37. Only Debbie Denton, a little Protestant girl of about four, lifted our unselfconscious cross-community spirits by singing 'The Sash' very badly indeed and then, with staggering nonpartisan versatility, producing another brand-new and previously unreleased epic about an IRA jailbreak from Mountjoy. Where she heard that one I'll never know.

— Up went the helicopter! she sang with great tuneless excitement. Up went the helicopter!

As the Head of Religion from London correctly observed, what a fascinating society.

9

The Action Man, the jointed, stiff-handed doll with the scar on his cheek, had to be decommissioned. Over the years he had rampaged as Australian bushranger, US Marine, French Foreign Legionnaire and Nazi staff officer, and now in the embarrassed end he had to go. It was a solemn moment. I loaded up his Sten guns, bazookas and Lugers, his grenades and daggers and bayonets, and laid him out on a ship of cardboard, squeezy bottles, sticks and fire lighters. On top of that his water bottle, his torches, his tools, his ammunition and the heap of jackets, jerseys, boots and the great orange parachute. Then very gently off the jetty, a match poked to the fire lighters, another match, a push and a Viking funeral for the Action Man off towards Valhalla or the Shannon. The blazing jumble bobbed out towards the Round O and on and on into the whirlpools and drags in the cool shade of the West Bridge, where it disappeared, smouldering, into the back of beyond.

Much had to be left behind or disposed of as I went to the big boys' classes and played in the big boys' yard. New demands were made. Reading whole books called novels. Looking up words in a dictionary – bad words. Talk of the 11-plus – the qually – and hard lads smoking ten a day down at Riverside. But not me, of course. Still a yella-belly, still behaving myself.

Change was slow and always far too late. It was confusion rather than anger that took root when I was slapped for not knowing what 'curiouser and curiouser' meant. I had suggested confidently enough, and with a certain justification, that it meant stranger and stranger.

— Yes, agreed the Brother, but what does it mean?

I thought for a moment.

— More weird and more weird?

— No.

The bamboo appeared.

— I'll give you one more chance.

I was completely bewildered. I knew I was right. I tried again.

— More bizarre and more bizarre?

— No. You don't know. Put out your hand!

The cane whistled and cracked off the ends of my fingers.

— The other one, said the red-faced Brother.

Whistle and crack and right across the knuckle of my thumb. I squeezed my smarting hands under my armpits and refused to cry.

— *Alice's Adventures in Wonderland*, he growled. Lewis
Carroll. Curiouser and curiouser.

Whether or not he explained further, I don't know, because I had stopped listening. How the hell was I supposed to know that? Only years later did it dawn on me what a warped exercise it had been for him to whack me across the fingertips with a stick for not spotting a literary reference from a book I had never read. I was only ten. For flip's sake!

By and large I got off very lightly, mainly because I was good at school. For the most part that just meant that I learnt my spellings the night before and so avoided the ritual punishment every morning. Words were called out from the spelling book and we wrote them down on strips of paper to be handed up and marked. And every morning without fail the same boys would get them wrong and would be cruelly tortured at the front of the class. Worse again, the rest of us were encouraged to look down on the victims and even enjoy their torment. The same boys would be hauled up later to the blackboard to stare vacantly at a long-division that everybody knew they would never in a million years or month of Sundays be able to work out. Hours were spent at this carry-on and, as with most classroom ceremonials, it took advantage of the fact that we were docile, frightened and too small to kick back. Too innocent, even, to appreciate that it was, in fact, damnable injustice. Too conditioned to ever refuse to put out the hand to be punished for our failings and inabilities, whether it be curiouser and curiouser, dyslexia or simply coming from a house where nobody got around to checking if you'd learnt your spellings or not.

Slowly, however, classroom rebellion and divilment grew. No longer was it enough to command that we put down our heads and be quiet when the teacher left the room. Teacherless classrooms now became scenes of ferocious bedlam. Flying books, compasses, rulers, pea-shooters and dirty books. There were fights, singsongs, trouserless dancers and animal noises. Most memorable of all was one bizarre Primary Seven moment when a certain exhibitionistic yahoo, prompted more by available colours than by any latent unionism, painted his penis red, white and blue. Now there was a strange one.

I was far too well-behaved, however, and only ever got in trouble on the odd occasion. There was one episode when I had heard a stupid joke the night before and suddenly remembered it again in class. I smiled quietly to myself, was caught doing so, and the teacher asked me what I thought was so funny.

— Nothing, Master.

He then announced that people who laugh at nothing would need to be careful because men with white coats would come and take them away. That was worrying. Men with white coats? Milkmen? Doctors? The same people who made the Bionic Man?

(The joke, by the way, was about a wee boy who asks the teacher can he go to the toilet and the teacher says he must say the alphabet first. The boy slowly and painstakingly recites the alphabet leaving out the letter P. 'Where's the P?' asks the teacher. And the wee boy says, 'Halfway down my leg.' Not a great joke but it made me smile then. I was only a cub – keeping my eye out for men in white coats.)

Then there was the time I was about to be punished along with a whole line of ragged convicts. I'm sure we had done something outrageous. Perhaps we'd been unable to spell 'delicatessen' or explain fully a simple concept like transubstantiation, or list the twelve apostles

without stuttering. Peter, Andrew, James and John. Philip,
Bartholomew, Matthew, Thomas, Simon, James, Jude and
Judas. Whatever the crime, I whispered to Marty Roche:

— Japers, we're in for it now!

The teacher fired a fearsome look along the line.

— Who said that?

Awkward endless silence.

— Was it you, Kelly? What did you say?

— I said, 'Japers, we're in for it now.'

— No you did not!

— Yes I did, Master.

There was no talking to him. He was convinced I had
said not 'japers' but 'Jaysus' and a metre stick began to
swing venomously through the air as we were picked off
one by one, our burning fingers turning blue, bony and
inconsolable.

And always gazing out the window at crows in the silent
playground, jackdaws, magpies, rooks, and Caesar Curry.
Out the snowy window, Lexington Avenue and the
beautiful Chrysler. As someone in the bar just said, the
most elegant building that ever walked. Walter Chrysler's
one-thousand-foot monument from 1930 that gives me my
bearings and keeps me right and reassured. And in all
directions, all the buildings I could ever see and imagine I
could see. The Rockefeller Center, the International
Building, the Grand Hyatt Hotel, the Daily News, the
Flatiron, Beekman, the Waldorf-Astoria, the Time Life, and
the powerful, evocative and hypnotic Empire State on the
corner of Fifth and Thirty-third. Once the tallest building in
the world (and now, I believe, number three), it has, I
confess, as much resonance for me as any Newgrange or
Navan Fort. And this is surely no surprise, for the Empire
State Building has towered in my imagination for as long

as I can remember. Read about in school, talked about in the yard, and framed in every shot. The great and unbelievable skyscraper in America scaled by King Kong, Fay Wray screaming, and in real life crashed into by a B-52. This was a building we always wanted to see for ourselves, like the Colosseum, the Eiffel Tower and Devenish. It was a definite place of pilgrimage, divine power, and a deep sense of the ultimate.

New York is all landscape. Like the geometrical pictures we created on graph paper and called 'patterns', it is all shape and symmetry. Brick, steel, glass, mirror, advert, neon and the yellow river of cabs cascading through the canyons. Endless vistas from one tunnelled end of an avenue to its disappearing horizon a million miles away. All perspective. All straight lines except for the people splashed and throbbing, always moving, honking and bouncing along, unstoppable. In this landscape you walk like a fast-talking, fast-thinking, buzzing, living thing. High on it. Invigorated by it. Picking up on every smell from every deli. Hearing every note of every passing tune and letting them all shoal together in your head to make your very own jazz. As alive and tuned in as a hare or a wolf. Hip-hop making perfect sense. Greg Osby blasting through a wire fence on Canal Street. Thelonious Monk. Miles. Bird. Public Enemy raging: 'Don't believe the hype! Don't, don't, don't believe the hype!'

And then back to the careless industry. The view from a hotel window always gets the better of me and so, charged up and sleepless, I write reams and reams and reams.

In school I once drew a landscape of Enniskillen. It was a view from the water, the whole town visible in silhouette against the sky. The town hall, the church spire, the

chapel's bulk, Cole's Monument, the mountains. This was
my childhood skyline and yet for some reason I added, as a
joke, the Empire State Building teetering magnificently on
the Diamond and the Statue of Liberty plonked like a
carnival float on Irvine's Island. Nobody could make head
nor tail of it. Only the discovery of a school-book
reproduction of Magritte's *Personal Values* provided the
relief of definition. It was straightforward. I was a ten-year-
old surrealist from Fermanagh – and proper order too.

The landscape of childhood was a varied one. Tarmac,
concrete, pebble dash and clay. From my bedroom
window I could see Derrygore and its nightly sunsets
over whin bushes, rushes and motionless cattle. It was a
bright and ever-changing hill under rolling, bruised clouds
and biblical light, and it swept with the lushest meadows
to the glassy lough.

Behind the estate, the Mill (or Racecourse) Lough, full of
pike and grebe, the drumming snipe and the heron. A huge
lake that gave me bulrushes and alders and sallies.
Bullfinches in the briars and swallows skimming their
own reflections. The stream full of water hens, baldies and
lazy old roach. Everywhere water. Flowing water, still
water, stagnant water. Grey water, sky-cloud water and
green water. Water bubbling with big-lipped bronze bream
and tiger perch. Eels wrapped around weeds and rusted
prams. Pike eating rats and scaldies, back-facing teeth that
would go right through your boot. Swifts screeching over
the roof tops and house martins attacking their mud nests
under the bridge. Swans doing as they were bid. The
astonishing turquoise kingfisher making a break for it. The
giant dragonfly. The midges. The cuckoo. The corncrake.

I hoked and poked in everything. I knew close up the
hard clay beaten into short cuts over fields. I knew the

sudden, scuttling, shocked activity under a turned rock – ants, slaters, centipedes, creepy-crawlies. Blades of grass were lush and full of daddy-longlegs, frogs and spiders. Seeds of grass were planed off in the hand and scattered like the feathers of pish-the-beds, clocks to tell the time. Nettles on the legs. Dockens. The nip of nectar in the clover and the honeysuckle. The reek of fungus and the scrunched-up leaf. Itchy-pees, blackberries, haws.

And then there was the smell of my own knees, all grass and dry mud and always bleeding. My hands full of thorns and splinters and deep clean cuts on razor reeds that made the best and shrillest calls. On my belly, eye to eye with bees and bugs and beetles, worms, leatherjackets and slugs. Running hard through the quicksand, glarry bog or the bumpy paupers' graveyard. Thin ice on the Mill Lough. Skimming stones. Sneaking up on larks. I was Tarzan, Geronimo, Cúchulainn, Zorro and Robin Hood. I knew myself, my knees, my distance and my patch. Never more aware of my wants and my wounds. Limestone and glar and sucking, squelching watery muck to fill the bubbling laceholes of gutties and baseball boots.

The yard was coal and coal dust. Briquettes and sticks. Hydrangea, geranium and rambling rose. Potato peelings and the smell of cabbage from the steamy kitchen window. Sparrows and chaffinches on the clothesline and the coal man humping sacks on his leathery back. The bread man conjuror sliding out his glorious trays of bread. The Maine man with his crates of raspberryade. A ritual Saturday morning procession of farting, hissing lorries out the back. Cidona. The ball stuck on the garage roof with the severed limbs of dolls, old anoraks and trainers, and Caesar Curry arriving on his imperious morning walk.

I was making things out of plastic bottles and coat

hangers. They squirted water and spun and when I was asked what they were, I said they were 'inventions'. And on Thursday nights the air-raid siren of the fire station wound up and down again, and I arranged stools and chairs around me and drummed along with rulers to Mud and Showaddywaddy and stared in deepest wonder at Pan's People. Babs. The blonde one.

School proceeded with more rigmarole than ever. Practice tests for the qually. Eye tests. Dean Flanagan arrived every week and said 'Good morning' and handed over his red-lined hat. He talked away and then asked us had we any questions and we would fire jokes at him.

— What's green and skips across Australia? Do you give up? Skippy the cooking apple!

In the dining hall cooks and supervisors held small upside-down boys by the ankles as they choked on their dinner, and we all went *woooooooohh!* when anybody dropped a plate. Tyres were let down. Boys schemed school and Sam Ferguson brought in his brother's Penny Black to show to us. It was worth a whole pile of money and we were impressed. Priceless, he said.

We sat the qually and there was a hard question on it. The answer was 'galleon' and only a couple of us got it right. Some boys had been promised racing bikes if they passed. Then we had to do the qually again because there had been a cock-up. Water off a duck's back. Whatever the case, that was suddenly the end of that.

On the last day at school we went on a nature walk around Riverside and there was a dead cat in the hedge. Coltsfoot, celandine, cow parsley, kidney vetch and goosegrass. Back in class the teacher gave us chocolate biscuits and lemonade and wished us well. Prayers were said and home we went, like ignorant little soldiers off to the front. One last summer to be the innocent Apache, Tom Sawyer, Davy Crockett and the Flashing Blade. Collect bumbly-bees in a jam jar and let them go again.

10

And while all of this was going on in Enniskillen, County Fermanagh (Northern Ireland, North of Ireland, Ulster, the Six Counties, the Sick Counties), Ireland, Europe, The World, The Universe et cetera, the planet earth was revolving away on its axis like an orange in a sheugh.

The 173rd Airborne in Vietnam, Clay hammered Liston again, Che Guevara, Clay beat Patterson, Rhodesia and UDI, Arkle won the Gold Cup three years in a row, Dylan went electric, napalm, Nobby Stiles won the World Cup, the Cultural Revolution, Eleanor Rigby, Muhammad Ali was stripped of his title, Celtic won the European Cup, the Six-Day War, Biafra, Martin Luther King was murdered,

Manchester United won the European Cup, Bobby
Kennedy was murdered, the Prague Spring, Tommy Smith
and John Carlos, Nixon, civil rights, the first man on the
moon, British troops, Manson, the Ho Chi Minh Trail,
Cambodia, the Beatles split, Brazil won the World Cup, de
Gaulle died, decimal currency, Idi Amin, Brian Faulkner,
Arsenal won the Double, internment, Louis Armstrong
died, Bloody Sunday, Watergate, bombs, Picasso died,
Yom Kippur, West Germany won the World Cup, Nixon
resigned, Lord Lucan, Duke Ellington died, Thatcher,
Beirut, Angola, Doctor Herrema, Franco died, Lester
Piggott won the Derby again, Mao died, Jimmy Carter,
the Sex Pistols and Red Rum.

In 1977, as I got ready for the big boys' school, Elvis
Presley was found dead at Graceland. The granny stood at
the jarbox and said:.

— Poor Elvis – gone but not forgotten.

11

The teacher who played the piano had yellow hair and smoked like a train. He arrayed his butts, upright, in little avenues on top of the piano and he could light a fresh fag without ever missing a beat. I sang away half-heartedly and watched him construct his miniature smouldering Manhattan, the longest silvery ash of the Chrysler Building always about to topple onto Lexington and the sleeves of his sheepskin coat. He was a decent spud.

And so to that instantly recognisable character – the Catholic boys' grammar school. The college, known to the older citizens who had paid for it as the seminary, was a huge hospital of a building which faced Hillview across the lough, its vacuous windowed façade catching the light at odd times of day. St Michael's Grammar School. St Mick's, the backdrop to seven years, the weird years of puberty, adolescence, change, catching myself on, and the long, gloomy descent into cynical, grown-up knowledge. A school no doubt the same as any other of its genre and well described by my fellow inmate Séamas Mac Annaidh as 'a red brick institution for the promotion of Gaelic football'.

In later years myself, Mac Annaidh and others had a rule (and I believe it still stands) that the first to bring up the subject of school had to buy the drinks. We knew that to mention any incident at all was to raise the dead, conjure angels and unleash outrageous spirits. The discussion was always inevitable and with the predictable repetition of the relieved, bitter and bereaved, exactly the same. With all the black humour of survivors, we would rehearse every detail once again – every injustice, every sign of madness, every long-embellished yarn. Impersonations, nicknames and regrets, and the sad feeling that if only we had been in our twenties as opposed to pubescent and screwed up, we wouldn't have stood for any of it. Certainly not be at the mercy of some institutionalised smart-ass who could only work his powers of wit on nervous twelve-year-olds.

As Mac Annaidh plopped peanuts from a great height into his tomato juice, I would again resign myself to paying for every round. Ritual. Therapy. A necessary working-out of the thing. Do you remember the time ...?

The most damnable act of oppression ever was when they started banning hymns. Catholic ethos, where are you! They banned a hymn. It was an uproarious martial rebel-rouser of a thing called 'Faith of Our Fathers',

old-fashioned even then and more than a touch defiant.
But here it was proscribed, outlawed and *ex cathedra* put
on the index by one of the infallible fathers. Whatever
next? Strange that they should ban a hymn, wouldn't
you think? Oliver Cromwell wouldn't be in it. For all its
orare, studere, agere, here we had the alma mater banning
a hymn which had been perfectly acceptable for years.
For generations it had closed all religious feasts and holy
days of obligation, sung by a gymful of eager boys,
cherubim and seraphim, ready for anything in spite of
dungeon, fire and sword.

— Dungeon, fire and sword and strap, says Mac
Annaidh.

— Oh don't start me talkin'.

The reason why St Michael's Grammar School banned
'Faith of Our Fathers' was a simple one. The gym had, as
you might expect, a polished wooden and very resonant
floor and 'Faith of Our Fathers' (good tune that it is) made
five hundred pairs of feet stamp and tramp in riotous
togetherness *con tutta forza.* That amounts to one thousand
feet, one thousand soles, one thousand heels and ten
thousand toes, many in tipped brogues for sparking
pavements outside Corrigan's, Tyler's, Flanagan's and
Sloan's. The resulting noise was not a marching sound as
such – not so much Roman legions or storm-troopers or
boy scouts or grenadier guards, more a Dubliners concert,
the Clancys perhaps, or God forbid, the Wolfe Tones.
'Faith of Our Fathers' is that kind of tune, and so its
imprimatur was revoked – the whole shooting gallery,
bell, book and candle. And some of us (*semper fideles*)
stopped stamping.

A wicked laugh from Mac Annaidh and he stamps his
feet,

We will be true to thee till death,
We will be true to thee till death.

He rubs his hands together.

— *Reality*, he says with great gravitas, *Reality* was a stupid magazine they always made us read. A Redemptorist publication, I believe.

— You're damn right! I agree with enthusiasm, and with an outrageous misnomer!

Looking back, I wonder if it was ever banned at all. Or are we imagining the whole thing? A bad dream?

To write about my seven years at St Mick's might well be a pointless exercise. It has all been done before – and done better. John Montague, who was at St Pat's in Armagh in the 1940s, concludes rather succinctly in his poem 'Time in Armagh' that 'A system/without love is a crock of shite.' I can't top that. And worse again, there's Joyce to live up to and live with. What student didn't make an innocent act of self-aggrandisement on reading *A Portrait of the Artist as a Young Man* when the young Dedalus is on the receiving end of the pandybat? And what aspiring writer can ever forget the admiration and the accompanying kick in the teeth that comes from the immediate revelation that he or she could never, in a fit, describe a beating with such clarity and perfection? We all knew a Baldyhead Dolan. We all still remember the feel of his fingers as he steadied your hand before the swish and crack of pandybat, metre stick, bamboo, wooden block or strap, and your own innocent hand crumpling 'like a leaf in the fire'.

To write about seven years of school and dwell on the grim would be wrong. I was reasonably successful in dealing with most of its disciplines. I applied the staying-out-of-bother skills I had learnt in primary school and got through most of its weirdnesses unscathed. Doing the homework, backing the books and learning the spellings was generally enough to keep them off your back. A rebellious youth would be doomed and many, of course, were.

To write here and now about teachers would be indulgent and in some cases downright malicious and so I'll resist abusing my privilege and exacting sweet-and-sour revenge. Nor would it be my wish to tar everyone with the same sweet-and-sour (and bitter) brush. Some of the teachers and priests were mannerly and civilised, some of them even sensitive, who inspired in me a sort of sympathy and respect. Some, too, were encouraging and got me through certain O-levels and A-levels, and for that I must be grateful. No point now in biting the hand that fed me mince and semolina for seven long years. There *was* good stuff too.

The night I first got at *Dubliners*, I read 'The Sisters' and wondered with great disappointment what all the fuss was about. This man Joyce was supposed to be good grown-up stuff. The next day the teacher talked about symbolism and twinkling rivers and paralysis, and everything suddenly clicked into place. For the first time, I felt consciously that I was off the blocks, as much to that teacher's credit as to Joyce's. Wilfred Owen, Hopkins, Wordsworth and later, *as Gaeilge*, Ó Ríordáin and Ó Direáin. And best of all, that first encounter with Heaney – 'Personal Helicon', 'Blackberry-Picking' and 'Mid-Term Break'. Seamus on the cover in his big duffel coat, welcoming us all to our own place. Science is ballocks, I decided. Now we're talkin'! Now we're motorin'! Here's something I actually *want* to read.

St Michael's Grammar School was a single sex, single religion holding centre where we were singularly encouraged to play shirtless Gaelic football on an all-weather pitch. (Typical of the place, however, the all-weather pitch had only the one kind of weather – hailstorms – first two periods on desolate Monday mornings.)

As in any institution, logic and sense very often went out the window and the torturous surrealism of dogma took over. A hard station, therefore, for a human being. A breeding ground, ironically, for a deeply subversive integrity. Not a quality of much use in Thatcher's workplace, but a good one even so.

On our first days we were initiated into the institution by gangs of culchie hallions who stuck our heads down toilets and under taps – a coarse baptism known as 'ducking'. The hallions all had long hair, sideburns, tight jumpers and flares, and looked like the men on the television who marched around Belfast with cudgels. They're probably all solicitors now – or teachers – maybe even priests. Big hoors we called them. Volcanic faces and yellow teeth.

Before we even got to school we were beaten men, weighed down by school bags, plastic bags and sports bags that we literally trailed along the ground behind us as we staggered along the black path and up the avenue to school in the rain. It was all right for the doctors' sons and the toffs from the Sligo Road who got dumped at the door in flash cars, but for the rest of us each day began with the agony of the avenue, the bags of books dragged up the mountain like a cruel and unusual penance, the wet clothes, the green radiators and pipes, the hallion prefects and the endless muttered prayers – act of this, act of the other, faith, hope and charity, no less! And all before classes had even started. Alarm bells. The press of a button. The newness of timetable, slippery corridors, moustachioed teachers, subjects from Mars – Latin, physics, chemistry – everything new and totally bewildering. And then the gullible sent off to get the keys of the handball alleys. The green. The innocent. The children in their outsize blazers and mid-grey trousers out of Tully's, red-faced and sweating. At the mercy of the whole thing.

All of a sudden, already-prepared genitals were revealed on the roller-blind blackboard. Male and female. In the biology textbook there was a chapter about a thing called 'reproduction'. Pictures of hens doing it, elephants doing it, rhinoceroses doing it, and an incomprehensible cross-sectional drawing that might well have been the dirty deed itself. (Not that any of it was at all clear.) The *what?* question could only be answered by confused private study of the chapter. The *how?* question could only be answered by the remarkably well-executed diagrams in Biro on the apple-stinking desks. The *when?* question, it appeared, could *never* be answered, and the *who with?* question simply did not apply.

Sex was explained as follows. The teacher went red in the face.

— Some of the farmers may know this already, he said. But can a calf be born just like that? I mean, can a cow just have a calf?

Mickey McCluskey put up his hand and explained that you needed a bull.

The headmaster (known as the president) then talked to everyone individually about what we were starting to call the birds and the bees. This interview consisted of him asking me had I any questions about what I had been learning in biology class, and me, of course, saying no (which was a very large lie). He then asked if, in that case, I understood what the Immaculate Conception meant. I lied again. So ended the formal sex education. To the ancient and obscene graffiti artists of previous generations, I am therefore most grateful for the Biro Kamasutra engraved with patient skill on the inky desks.

And then the school slipped up badly. I think it was as a reward for a charity walk that we were paraded one afternoon to the Ritz to see a movie called *Midnight Express*. There was great excitement – a whole afternoon off school to go to the pictures to see a cowboy picture, a train robbery or perhaps an Agatha Christie. At least that's what *Midnight Express* sounded like to us. The authorities were being unnervingly generous and we all sat down with our innocent bags of Tayto.

It didn't take long to realise the mistake. This was no cowboy movie, train robbery or Agatha Christie. This was an extremely adult Alan Parker thriller about an American drug smuggler having a tough time of it in a Turkish prison. A very bad word – the whole word – suddenly echoed off the walls and we immediately knew we were on to something. This was an X! The language got worse, there was a ferocious, bloody and unforgettable fight and next thing there were two soapy men snogging in a shower. You can imagine the remarks shouted from the darkness by our riotous contingent of homophobic youth. And who was going to explain this one once the mammies and the daddies found out?

Then it really got going. Out of the blue, the prisoner's girlfriend arrived in the visiting area, opened her blouse and pressed her memorable breasts up against the glass partition. It was quite an effect. They say the dean tried to jump up and block the projector's rays, but I can't be sure of this. The screen had my full attention. The prisoner, who by this stage was completely mad, pressed his face against his side of the glass and drooled. We drooled, too.

— He might be mad, yelled a seventh year, but he's one of us!

I haven't been the same since.

When writing about school, the danger of exaggeration is a real one. Michael Dinner's movie *Catholic Boys* is certainly full of truths, but it does not reflect my experience. I was never in my life separated from a girl while slow-dancing to 'Wonderful Tonight' at a school disco. No nuns with rulers, no telephone directories for girls to sit on, no reflections in patent leather shoes. But then again, maybe I was never in the sort of clinch that merited ecclesiastical interference. By the time we got to disco age we were not tortured so much by this sex-is-a-sin palaver as by the fact that occasions of sin, never mind actual sins, were apparently impossible to arrange. The feel of the material of a girl's duffel coat as you walked her nowhere in particular would have to be pleasure enough. And anyway, by the time we got into any kind of contact with girls we were all pubescent crazy-heads – all spots and delusions and entirely incapable of engaging a girl in basic conversation let alone anything more intimate.

That it was an all-boys' school made things worse. There we were developing bizarre notions and attitudes towards the opposite sex without much intercourse – of any kind – with the real thing. All very well to swagger about the corridors all day long, thinking about girls and talking about girls and perhaps even under the illusion that you were actually going out with a girl, when, in reality, you didn't even *see* one from one end of the day to the other. Segregation, therefore, made that lost hour after school a rare spectacle. Boys and girls waited for yellow buses to take them to far-flung corners of the county and the odd awkward collision between the sexes might occasionally occur. It usually amounted to slagging, name-calling and possibly, if you were lucky, a type of half-hearted embarrassed wrestling. Innocent, confused, hormone-fuelled excitement, and with no apparent purpose.

The annual opportunity to wrestle with girls was at the *feis* – a word which, among other things, means 'sexual intercourse', according to Ó Dónaill. In this very particular case, however, it was a musical gathering in the technical college, with Sister Aquinas acting as bouncer – a series of competitions and adjudications where schools were pitted against one another and seven hundred girls got up, one after another, with daft expressions on their faces and sang Percy French songs, listened to only by their gruesome parents and the odd nun. The highlight, however, was the choir competition, where we took on our female equivalent, Mount Lourdes Convent Grammar School – an event which, by no particular design, always seemed to coincide with the Aintree Grand National.

We were spotless in those days, boy sopranos who laughably believed that we might have something to offer what we called 'the talent'. Our nascent masculinity was manifested in the strange Ninja ritual of tying our school ties around our heads. This, we believed, made us somehow attractive. On stage we stood on treacherous benches, a whole choir of aspiring men herded by a priest who believed in us as much as he believed in God. His hands balanced us, conducted us and, between songs, prayed for us in case we'd all tumble or go flat. He was very proud of us in our tearful harmonies, singing bits of *La Traviata*, rampant songs of life and lust in some weird, sinless sound. Gregorian chant, the Kyrie, sad songs in

Irish about Feidhlimí's boat going down on the way to Góla. It would have broken your heart, right enough.

But the singing was secondary and we always took our eyes off the conducting priest for the whiteness of dresses at the door, Mount Lourdes girls in one exotic sweep from the convent to the Pyrenees, all of them smelling of roses and chewing gum. All we could do was elbow each other off the stage and wrestle a bit, anything but talk to these dangerous angels. Trail them sadly around the building and wait to have our voices and our hearts broken naturally. When they passed by we would talk loudly about bookies' shops and horses. Crisp, L'Escargot and Red Rum.

To think that in the hotel this evening a real live Manhattan hooker had slipped her calling card under my door. If I'd been twelve years old I'd have invited her in, sat her down on the edge of the bed and asked her a series of pertinent questions.

— OK, Miss, I know about hens and elephants, and I know you need a bull – but what I need to know is this –

S t Michael's brought together a rare selection of people. First of all there was the urban and the rural, and that produced an immediate clash. Townies like myself were looked down upon by country people as corner boys, and country people were themselves looked down upon by the townies as culchies. Hovering wealthily over all of this were the business people, the merchant classes with money to burn, and they looked down on everybody. These, of course, are sweeping generalisations but there is some truth in them. For the well-to-do, the college was almost an inevitability. Older brothers had all attended and their pedigree was often proclaimed. Is it unfair to suggest that the purpose of the place was simply to churn out respectable middle-class Catholics? Ranks of solicitors, doctors, teachers and priests? Whatever. That was never my particular milieu.

A friend who attended a similar establishment recalls his headmaster out blessing parents' cars – but only the expensive ones, mind you – liberally splashing holy water over lines of Mercedes owned by chemists, dentists, lawyers, publicans and car dealers. It's always as well to keep in with the gentry. You never know when you'll need a good lawyer – or a car dealer.

This is not to say that I was the working-class hero persecuted among the toffs, but I did encounter attitudes that were unfamiliar. Right-wing attitudes about money and work and a contempt for both the working man and the unemployed man. Not among teachers but among the pupils themselves, repeating faithfully the crude politics of their parents, who were finding a warped heroine in Downing Street in 1979. All Thatcher did was ignite it. Northern towns, for all their decency, are also full of snobbery. If you came from Kilmacormick or Cornagrade or Hillview, you weren't considered to be of quite the same calibre as people from Drumclay, Old Rossorry or the Sligo Road. Nor were you expected to do as well. Money certainly meant privilege, although it was clear from early on that it didn't mean brains. With this in mind, I tried my very best to remain well-balanced, with a chip on both shoulders, as they say.

So school was quite a mulligan stew, all of it stirred occasionally by a contingent of priests from Monaghan who were a million miles from Kent Plastics, Tunney's Meat Packers or Ulster Swifts. No notion. For me, setting foot in the grammar school (with every intention of staying) had propelled me into a different but not necessarily better orbit.

I also knew very well that I was only at the grammar school because I had passed the 11-plus. There were many like me and being thrown in with boys who would one day inherit the daddy's business only served to make me more aware of myself and my own background. The more I looked around me, the more I became deeply proud of where I had come from.

There was one tribal bind that, notionally, held us together. We were all supposed to be Catholics. St Michael's or St Anybody's, as any northerner will tell you, is a giveaway. Segregated education was the order of the day. No mixing with girls and definitely no mixing with people of other religions, at least during school hours. After school, of course, we all integrated ourselves perfectly for the sake of company, football or romance.

Our opposite numbers attended Portora Royal School, a place for which I have a strange affection and loyalty if only for the fact that both Oscar Wilde and Samuel Beckett were pupils there. The hardy Beckett used to go for an early morning swim down behind the granny's house and doubtless the young Oscar, in his boater, was harangued by some of my yahoo ancestors as he promenaded with great style along the Brook. Indeed Mac Annaidh on his first television interview made me smile by wearing a Portora tie, a wonderful piece of subversive mischief – and he knew damn well what he was doing.

Separate schooling did not have the same sort of effect that it may have had in other northern towns and the town itself was never a heavy sectarian spot. True, the school was Catholic in ethos (whatever that means) but it was, in fairness, never a bigoted place and there was never any anti-Protestant propaganda in my hearing. Ecumenism was the thing and a Presbyterian minister came to explain what it was. So no tales of two schools throwing stones at each other. That we were situated close to the Collegiate was a further occasion of proof that sectarianism was never a dominant force. All those legions of Protestant girls were no less attractive than their Catholic counterparts. In fact two St Mick's boys had some early degree of success and triumphantly wore Collegiate scarves to school, perfumed trophies of the girls they met off yellow buses from Kesh and Ballinamallard every morning.

Again it was a class thing. The irony is that it would be far more likely for boys and girls from St Michael's and Mount Lourdes to attend or be invited to formals in Portora and the Collegiate than it was for them to have much social intercourse with the secondary schools. As Mac Annaidh has observed, grammar schools are usually built on hilltops, secondary schools in bogs.

I went to Portora myself in a kind of a way. Every summer Portora's outdoor swimming pool was open to all-comers and I virtually lived in it. Long amphibious summers from early morning when the mist rose off the water to hot summer afternoons full of clegs and grass-hoppers and big impossible girls sunning themselves on towels.

Learning to swim had been another vital trauma. Conditioned by the granny not to go near the water, here I was suddenly up to my shins in the shallow end, awkward and shivering like a vexed white bird who could neither float nor fly. At the far end, where the pool was a deeper blue, the rest of them duck-dived for bricks, bombed and belly-flopped, butterflied and crawled and jackknifed like Tarzan from the highest board. I watched with envy and determination, and eventually pride made me float, leaning into nothing and kicking like a mad frog. Johnny Weissmuller. Mark Spitz. Teddy Keenan, a local hero I watched swim to the horizon and back at Bundoran. I started with inflatable orange armbands and mouthfuls of chlorine. Then widths, then into the middle, and finally the hundred yards, three lengths and a crazy leap into the bottomless deep end to prove you wouldn't panic. That was some launch, another of those necessary moments of abandon, another leaving behind.

And then after the holidays back to St Mick's to walk on the right-hand side of the corridor with your bag over your left shoulder – this apparently to maintain the smooth flow of pupils and to preserve the walls. Maybe so, but it seemed to me like another rule to be enforced with the absurd logic of any dogma. Bold white lines appeared on the tarmac and we were told not to cross them. Nothing in particular seemed to exist beyond these white lines and so we naturally treated them with contempt. Red rag. Hurling ourselves at imaginary force fields, running hard at these invisible barriers and being continually thrown back (we were true believers in *Star Trek* if not in school rules). We pictured disintegrated schoolboys being scattered on the roses late at night and we warned of the peril the bishop would surely be in should he make a surprise visit. I was reaching the age where I realised that nonsense was the best way to deal with nonsense. I knew we had succeeded when the very man who had instituted these partitionist white lines observed our activity from his window, and while clearly wondering what exactly the future Catholic middle classes were up to, thought better of saying anything in reproach. A small victory.

What we were getting up to was, in fact, very small

potatoes compared to what some of the staff were at.
Picture the scene in among the wooden benches of the
chemistry lab.

A bellowing Cork accent.

— Belly in! Chest out! Feet at angle of forty-five degrees!

The boys are then lined up along the wall for a rigorous
inspection involving constant references to the Gestapo,
Hermann Goering, Rudolf Hess and A-dolf Hitler. Nazi
salutes follow and eventually class begins. Chemicals are
heated on Bunsen burners and the goggled teacher is
visibly delighted as they assume the colours of various
hurling counties. On a nearby Bunsen burner, Heinz beans
bubble slowly in the tin.

Looking back on this particular scenario, I am quite
baffled. We were too young and stupid to understand
that such Nazi shenanigans were, to say the least, rather
inappropriate. We just thought it was funny. It took a
French teacher to put us right, objecting very strongly and
quite rightly to the swastikas we ignorantly planting
on his blackboard with six stamps of a chalky wooden
duster. Whether or not that Hitler stuff was all part of some
kind of joke, I don't know. Certainly strange. Certainly
very hard to explain.

More Cork roaring and a baseball bat smashes down on
the desk.

— The colour of the third-best hurling team in Ireland –
what colour is that, boy?

— Purple, sir!

— 'Tis not purple, boy! 'Tis maroon! And who wears
maroon, boys?

— Galway, sir!

— Yes, Galway, the third-best hurling team in Ireland. And what colours are these? The colours of the second-best hurling team in Ireland?

— Orange and black, sir!

— No – 'tis not orange, boy, 'tis amber.

— Black and amber, sir.

— Exactly! And who wears the colours black and amber upon their backs, boys?

— Kilkenny, sir.

— *Kil*-kenny! *Pre*-cisely! The second-best hurling team in Ireland! And now, boys – finally – at last – what colour do you call that?

— Red, sir!

— Red! Red! Red! The colour of the best hurling team in Ireland! And who is the best hurling team in Ireland, boys?

— Cork, sir! Cork! Up Cork! Come on, Cork!

— Yes, boys! *Cark! Cark!* The best hurling team in Ireland! Now get out of my sight! Raus! Raus! Raus!

Curiouser and curiouser. It beats me.

There was a piano in the music room and that way lay salvation, sanctification and purification. Before class Kevin McVeigh took to belting out some rock-'n'-roll barrelhouse boogie, and it was the most wonderful noise ever heard by either of my two ears. We gathered around, and the same instinct that got Jerry Lee Lewis chucked out of Bible College in Waxahachie, Texas, was awakened in me and I began to hammer out notes up at the top. Fireworks. The clawed right hand of a demon. Here another liberation – beating the hell out of an upright Danemann – music like a thunderstorm – slates flying in all directions off my roof. GREAT BALLS OF FIRE! Of course

nothing as dramatic as all that happened. I was still, at the
back of it all, an uptight wee conservative fool who
thought too much about right and wrong and believed too
much in good taste and other people's notions. Only
gradually was rebellion seeping in and out. I read about
Karl Marx and got a Motorhead record out of the library. A
long way from the Angelus and the sweet ballads we were
winning cups for at the *feis*, but even so, I was still full of
quiet disapproval when fags were lit and jokes were made
about dead people. Far too grown-up and all of my
opinions both second-hand and erroneous. Self-education
was therefore required and wouldn't come until much
later. The turning point, perhaps, was Holy Thursday,
1980.

Thin Lizzy swept into Enniskillen in two Mercedes to play
a concert at the Lakeland Forum – or the Complex as we
called it. It was part of a world tour and a few small shows
around Ireland were the warm-ups before America, Japan
and the rest of Europe. I had *Live and Dangerous* on cassette
and listened to little else. 'The Boys are Back in Town'.
'Jailbreak'. 'The Rocker'.

At first, nobody believed they were actually going to
come. Surely a daft rumour, and there were whispers
about Hell's Angels and serious trouble. There had just
been a wild bust-up at a Toe-Jam gig in a marquee and
apparently it wasn't over yet because the Hell's Angels
were still miffed. I wasn't there myself but the next
morning, as I picked my way through burnt bikes and
scattered helmets, I could imagine that the Angels were
very sore.

It hadn't all been violence though. I'm told there was a
bizarre *Carry On* scene of mass trouser-hoisting when

somebody turned on the floodlights on the pitch. Imagine that in the Broad Meadow! Riots and open-air sex in Enniskillen on the same night! Whatever next? A drive-in Kentucky Fried Chicken?

Nobody like Thin Lizzy had ever come to Enniskillen. There was great excitement and sure enough, one morning on the way to school, there was a poster outside the meat factory: THIN LIZZY WORLD TOUR 1980 – LAKELAND FORUM, ENNISKILLEN. By teatime I had the pink ticket in my hand.

I went into that concert in a brown cardigan and I came out in a leather jacket. I'll never forget a minute of it. None of us had ever seen the like of it before. Explosions, lights, walls of Marshall amplifiers and Philip Lynott appearing through the smoke – this unlikely big black Dubliner in leather strides, foot up on the monitor, fist in the air and a mouthful of teeth that would blind you.

— This is for all you Enniskillen cowboys.

Everything was blasted away. It was as if a spaceship had landed like the one in *Close Encounters*, its door opened wide, and without giving it a second thought we had charged the light. It was as if my brain was some kind of photographic paper that night. Every image was flashed, developed and fixed in every sweaty, hoarse detail. When I meet other people who had been there too, I get the same story. Boy, did we need what we got that night.

The music was perfect for us. It was mostly hormone rock – power chords and driving beats – but there was also enough poetry and romance to keep it manageable. As much about the lonely cowboy missing his girl as the crazy wild man back in town who just wanted to party. At fifteen I wanted to be both. We formed bands and tried our damnedest to sound like Lizzy. Now and again we did. Usually we just sounded like acne.

Prior to that we had tried and failed to be Horslips at a school concert. I was hacking at a bass guitar and I was mortified because the guitar belonged to someone whose mother was into God and there was a sticker on it proclaiming: THE LORD IS MY SHEPHERD. No harm to her or the Lord, but it wasn't very rock-'n'-roll, was it? But then neither were we. For that premature appearance somebody had titled us the Golden Arrows, after the chip shop that belonged to the singer's family. It was a great chip shop run by Silvano Lucchesi, a grand and noble-looking man who often gave me free ice cream. The band, however, had few of the qualities of either Silvano or the chip shop, but I don't think we knew it at the time.

— A bit of Led Zeppelin for the boys at the back.

After that I got my own secular guitar and we found what we thought was a much better name – Tangent. God save us! Tangent! Murdering songs by Rush and Rory Gallagher and opening for Mama's Boys in St Ronan's Hall. It was entirely hormonal.

I never missed a Thin Lizzy tour. Off to the RDS and rock festivals at Slane and Castlebar. Long expeditions by bus and by train. Lost in Dublin and sleeping on floors. Buying the T-shirts and finally tracking them all down in the Bailey on the night they played their very last show in Dublin. In later years the first interview I ever did was with Phil. I have a photograph of the two of us on my wall. Philip Lynott with his arm around my shoulder.

At that last Lizzy show in Dublin I had *my* arm around someone's shoulder. I had a girlfriend! I often wonder how I ever managed it. Perhaps perseverance on my part and martyrdom on hers? I was in those days what my father would call 'a right-lookin' sketch'. I always dressed in a green army jacket, T-shirt, drainpipe black jeans with a big belt, and incredibly large white baseball boots. My hair was as long as school rules would allow and there was usually one scabby spot somewhere obvious on my face – like right between the eyes. Worse again was the headless spot on the swollen, unsqueezable end of the nose. That was a real bastard that one. To summarise, I was no oil painting and I had all the physical charm of a pipe cleaner. My Derrygonnelly girlfriend, however, was good-looking and sought-after and presumably went out with me out of a sense of big-hearted charity. I am still grateful to her and learnt early on that women are much more gracious and open than the fascist hordes of men who seek perfection even when it's already breathing in their ears.

I asked her to the formal and she said yes. Yes, she said, yes. The Rascals played 'Three Times a Lady'. I looked ridiculous. I met her after school and plucked her and her constant friends from the gushing river of turquoise and purple that flowed out the gates of Mount Lourdes at half-past three. I walked her and her friends to the bus. She and her friends got on the bus and I phoned her later from a smelly phone box. Alone at last. I would tell about how I was reading *Ulysses* (and omit that I understood very little of it) and that Rory Gallagher was playing in Omagh.

Now and again gangs of us went to the Ritz to see *ET* or *An Officer and a Gentleman*. There were awful discos in the Killyhevlin or, if you were lucky, Rock Stewart and the Plattermen. The Memories in Bundoran – even Moving Hearts. She didn't like the Hearts and I just couldn't understand that. I decided that girls were weird, musically speaking. Just one of those things, I thought.

She went to France for the summer and when she came back she didn't want to go out with me any more. Quite right too. She should be canonised for having gone out

with me in the first place. Thank you. Thank you. Thank
you. Thank you. Thank you. And we're still in a relationship. These days she's my accountant – and a very good
one too.

etting to Broadway is a tall order for any writer at the best of times. To get there during a raging blizzard is damn near impossible, at least as difficult for those of us with tickets as it was for Brian Friel, whose *Molly Sweeney* was opening at the Roundabout Theater on the corner of Forty-fifth Street. I had been to a Broadway performance before – Stephen Rea and James McDaniel from *NYPD Blue* in Frank McGuinness's *Someone Who'll Watch Over Me* – but this was my first Broadway opening night and the blizzard made it all the more fascinating.

I remembered Brendan Behan's account of an opening night aftermath in Downey's, with Jason Robards, Lauren Bacall and Jackie Gleason. Gleason wanted to talk Irish and when Behan asked him (in Irish) how he was, Gleason replied (in Irish), one, two, three, four. No Behan or Gleason tonight, but Robards was in the cast, playing the dilapidated Donegal eye doctor.

With street signs covered in snow, the natural light fading and fresh snow literally up to your knees, the neon glare of Broadway was blinding and unreal. The Great White Way was for once deserted (and white) and there hadn't been a murder for days. Post-battle snowploughs lay abandoned outside porno theatres, betraying their drivers like horses outside pubs. Another planet entirely.

Inside the civilised Roundabout Theater I sat beside a civilised old New Yorker who went to plays all week long. He quizzed me about Donegal and Ballybeg and somehow we got on to Spencer Tracy. An unlikely couple in front were having a quiet but passionate row about understanding and commitment. There were tears. The world and his wife showed up and arrived like triumphant explorers. Pete and Fukiko, Scanlon, Breslin and McCourt, and I was dying of the cold. Carole King was humming a tune to my right. Carole King, no less. 'Will you Love me Tomorrow?', 'The Locomotion', 'Up on the Roof', 'Cryin' in the Rain', 'You've Got a Friend', 'Natural Woman'. The talent in the house tonight! And once more I inwardly declared that New York was one rare place. On top of that, the poet Heaney was a few rows back, being congratulated on a recent not inconsiderable achievement, and was giving me the thumbs up. All of us united as hardy transatlantic pilgrims who had braved a state of emergency to see a play.

Outside, Broadway was frozen like Walt Disney. Inside, Catherine Byrne, Alfred Molina and Jason Robards took us to Donegal and kept us there enthralled, in fits and in tears.

From Ballybeg to Broadway, the papers would say.

In Rosie O'Grady's we watched in disbelief as skiers flashed past the windows. Grub was ordered. The cast awaited the *New York Times* to come in across the snow. Runners were dispatched. Stories were swapped about Hammond, about Tyson, about Bacall, and, of course, about the price of a round in Stockholm. Very dear. That vodka is a catchpenny. On the long march home we were in bad need of a troika.

In bed, reeking of cigar smoke, dry-throated and full of the cold, I dreamt the recurring dream. I had an exam to sit. It was in maths or chemistry or physics or some other subject to which I have paid no attention since those corridor days on the hill. The exam is to be done that morning and I haven't done a tap. Nightmare.

— But I thought I was finished school? I protest.
— No you are not. You *thought* you were! You have been gallivanting around the place, putting off the inevitable. But now, my boy, you have to wise up and sit down and do the exam.
— But I haven't done a tap.
— Tough. You had plenty of warning. You knew you would have to do this exam but you have been raking around New York and now, my boy, it's time to pay the piper. Open your paper. Begin!

The panic gets the better of me and I waken up, genuinely relieved. It happens regularly enough. A vestigial fear of exams? Or is it worse than that? A Judgment Day complex, perhaps, and am I, without being aware of it, suffering from Catholic guilt after all – a condition I don't even recognise? It's a weird one and it's a recurring one. All my friends have the same trouble. Maybe I should ring Woody's analyst. Did I, after all, leave school with a silent A-level in guilt? Surely not? Surely guilt is a figment of the Irish writer's imagination? Surely a makey-up complex for good copy and an extra chapter? Not me, I'm from Fermanagh – straightforward and destined never to win a senior All-Ireland medal. No hang-ups in Fermanagh – only a sports complex.

Imagine going through all of this backward-looking palaver lying in the Manhattan scratcher on the flat of my back on a New York morning during the blizzard of '96 after a Broadway play and a long night in good company. Still can't get the school out of the system – and I'm thirty years old. Still no purge. No release. *Orare, studere, agere. Noli me tangere.*

In those days I had both the energy and the shamelessness to work within the system while at the same time keeping myself amused with what passed for subversion. Silly things like when I would be called upon to play the tin whistle at whole-school holy gatherings in the assembly hall – real Cecil B. de Mille productions with choirs, music and priests a-go-go. An irresistible scenario. 'Faith of Our Fathers' having been banned (the gerundive obligation), there grew a fad for slow airs to promote a feeling of meditative ease, and I was a man with a tin whistle in my inside pocket. My speciality was to make up airs as I went along but on one occasion I decided to play, at some solemn moment, a tune called 'Mná na hÉireann'. It's an old thing from the 1700s in praise of women and here I attempt a rough translation of some of the pertinent lines:

There's a woman who promised
that if I'd strayed with her

I'd get some gold.
And there's a woman in her nightgown,
more gorgeous than the other,
who teased Ballymoyer and the whole of Tyrone.
And there's no relief from this desperate torture
but a massive feed of drink.

I've been loose with Ó Doirnín but you get the idea.
Unfortunately so did the bishop, a Gaelic scholar who was
present to talk about vocations.

Arís, the school magazine, was another carefully
monitored opportunity for divilment. Subversion had to
be subtle, well-hidden among the poems, the annual report
from the chess club and accounts of gallant victories on the
sports field (often so hidden that only the editor knew it
was there at all). I was editor once and my appointment
had been a most outrageous abuse of the democratic
system. I had an election agent with unorthodox methods
and it seemed as if busloads of voters had been ferried in
from the surrounding countryside to exercise their fran-
chise early and often. What we had staged was a coup – a
sixth-form takeover of a seventh-form domain. Sheer
weight of numbers, mild bullying and dirty tricks. Never
had the English class seen so many enthusiastically
gathered and the room fair glittered with pioneer pins. I
thanked my campaign staff and, like Joe Stalin, took a good
long look at those who had opposed.

In the event, I filled the magazine with badly written
garbage about guitar players while others wrote poems
about virginal doves in odd moments of definite eroticism
(usually farmers who knew that you needed a bull et
cetera). I wrote some long-winded poem about Lough
Derg and I remember a phrase about a 'Holy Alcatraz'.

One of the teachers thought this was good and said I should write more.

My predecessor as editor was already writing more – five or six novels lay in scrawly file pages under the bed. Mac Annaidh was always perched somewhere with a milk bottle in one pocket and a tobacco tin containing a cheese sandwich in the other, a constant focus of madness and some kind of what I suppose was performance art. Not that we knew what performance art was. Still don't. One of his schemes was to run the stamp club, which meant carrying around a big book by Stanley Gibbons. Another involved fronting a punk band called Hot Vomit that didn't actually exist – he saw this as the logical response to punk rock. Mac Annaidh was recognised far and wide both as the Blackbird and as Rasputin.

Another sideline was his peculiar self-invented jazz dancing at the school disco – a bit of monthly excitement with vague possibilities. The floor would clear and the Russian cleric would position himself in the middle under the flashing lights and commence shimmying, shaking, buck-lepping, high-kicking, arm-waving, quivering, trapped-in-a-box miming, screeching and head-banging. *Saturday Night Fever* had nothing on Rasputin. It was frightening, bewildering and indescribable. Riverdance me arse!

Mac Annaidh was also one of two senior boys who wore beards. His was after the fashion of the Russian novelists (or mad clerics) and often provoked comment from the closely shaved religious.

— You'll have to remove that beard, Mac Annaidh.

— Why, Father? It's very nice, so it is.

— You're giving bad example to the first years.

— How am I giving bad example to the first years,

Father? They can't grow beards.

But while the Blackbird could put on an antic disposition and catch the conscience of the king, the rest of us weren't quite so clever and gradually turned into a herd of feral goats who head-butted everything in frustrated ignorance. One of our number suddenly stood up during an exam.

— Round the rugged rocks, the ragged rascal ran! he declared.

Some time later a postcard arrived with the news that he was relieving himself against the Berlin Wall. Perhaps the beginning of the end of the Cold War? I must ask him about it.

I managed not to do anything drastic or draw any particular attention to myself and drifted on. That I had my Derrygonnelly girlfriend was a definite stabiliser. That she was a normal, attractive human being and was prepared to be seen publicly with me must surely have made me a little more normal, easy and reassured. Maybe even less spotty.

Examinations were regular and torturous. If you did well in your exams you were a stew, and so I was therefore *technically* a stew – but I never, ever stewed. I hated stewing. I preferred listening to Dave Fanning on the radio, cramming and letting my granny do the novenas. There were other techniques, too, and the most frowned upon was coggin'. This involved copying from the person next to you, passing notes, smuggling in reams of information on tissue paper, arriving with essays already written out, hiding your textbooks in the cisterns, or decorating your own body with formulae and symbols like some tattooed South Pacific warrior to be read at leisure. Very few people attempted coggin' and even fewer with any success. I think we were all secretly against it. Anyone caught coggin' would be court-martialled and shot.

I remember one occasion when there was a bomb scare. This, after all, was the place called Northern Ireland and bomb scares had to be taken seriously. Pens down, everybody out, walk, don't run. We would assemble on the all-weather pitch and it was inevitable that someone might eventually enquire furtively what you'd got for question six?

— Why? What did you get for it?

But that wasn't the same as coggin'.

A-levels came and went. I was studying subjects I was reasonably good at and so I got through. There had been talk of careers but it all seemed a bit too serious, so I drifted through all that palaver without ever really engaging. But I liked the sound of four years of university – and I certainly had no better notions of my own.

On the last day at the Fun Palace I ran down the avenue with all the crazy freedom of a ski-jumper. The tie was off. The shirt was open. The books were buried. I took one final look back up the hill and made what seemed like the appropriate gesture. It was June, it was sunny, bees were in the clover and swallows and swifts swooped about my head. The hedges and the rushes smelt of a heavy green summer and I felt a definite conclusion had been reached. I had wised up. No more bullshit. No more bullshite.

Forgive the indulgence of a diary extract from that very day. Shows you the kind of balloon I was in those days, despite seven years of whatever it was.

Went home along the black path and noted that the fish were jumpin' and several of my friends were high. Into the house, stiff pure orange, removed the uniform and had a symbolic shower to cleanse myself. Off in the gondola and rendezvoused with other members of the

Fermanagh Renaissance under the East Bridge.

Brother Séamas's hat was offered in thanks to Pek, the Great Fish God of Lower Lough Erne, and we chanted 'Maguire! Maguire! Maguire!' as the hat floated in flames down the lough where it was apparently intercepted by an RUC submarine off the south-east coast of Devenish. We then perched like cormorants on the rocks, arms outstretched, and proposed a toast to the future and gulped our buttermilk with gusto (buttermilk with gusto on the rocks is a rare Fermanagh delicacy).

Into Mac Annaidh's cattle-cot, and punted our way to a certain school which was until that very day the place wherein lived the Cutties – a rare tribe of Fermanagh women of fine aspect and indelicate manner. There we met, as prearranged, with several of their number and presented them with offerings of boxty and cabbage. These they accepted as tokens of our almost entirely honourable intentions and they willingly joined us as we drifted off to another island where we literally burnt the books.

The ashes were put in a red plastic bucket with a white grip handle along with breadcrumbs, water and olive oil. The whole thing was then mixed into a thick dough and scattered in little lumps into the lough, where it was snapped up with vigour by throngs of cormorants, water hens, alligators and the odd brave fish. There then followed a ritual burning of school uniforms and a mad pagan festival in honour of Pek. This continued for three days and three nights with a lone piper keeping neighbouring islands awake and aware.

And that after seven years in a grammar school! Half of

Mac Annaidh's beard was ceremoniously shaved off and a notice was placed in the paper to announce that Mr Blackbird was dead.

On Broadway, Mr Friel's notices were, quite rightly, rather more positive than that.

14

And while all of this was going on in Enniskillen, County Fermanagh et cetera, the planet earth was still revolving away on its axis ...

The Boat People, bombs, *Saturday Night Fever*, the *Amoco Cadiz*, Mario Kempes, a test-tube baby, John Paul I, John Paul II, Jim Jones, Ayatollah Khomeini, Begin and Sadat, Abel Muzorewa, Thatcher, Sandinistas, bombs, the Popemobile, Iran, Afghanistan, Robert Mugabe, Moscow Olympics, J.R. Ewing, Reagan, John Lennon killed, Reagan shot, Pope shot, Hunger Strikes, Sadat killed, unemployment, Galtieri, Exocets, Paulo Rossi, Beirut, cruise missiles, bombs, Solidarity, bombs.

In 1983 Thatcher was re-elected and the television news

reran footage from 1979: 'Where there is discord may we
bring harmony ... where there is despair may we bring
hope.'

In Enniskillen, decent people were out of work and on
the dole for the first time in their lives.

15

Up and out for breakfast. There is nothing like a New York breakfast in the snow. Coffee, eggs, toast and cold water in a cloudy glass. Crispy, crispy bacon. The whole day and the whole city was mine and I was in the mood for limited exposure to art. The Metropolitan Museum of Art? The Frick Collection? The Whitney? The Guggenheim? I fancied a look at the Mondrian exhibition that was the current talk of the town and so I chose the Museum of Modern Art on West Fifty-third between Fifth and Sixth. You really ought to hear a New Yorker say 'Mondrian'. Or a Fermanagh man, for that matter.

There was a teenage time of even greater ignorance when I would have said things like, 'Picasso me arse!' But then the art got to work and I started to see things in a new way, or maybe even see things for the first time in *any* sort of way. This was another opening up, another freedom, and now in the Museum of Modern Art, I found myself standing spellbound in front of a huge Jackson Pollock, a man who had been easy for a schoolboy to abuse with such an irresistible rhyme available for his surname.

My eyes had been gradually opened by my father in the kitchen, by an art teacher at school, by Van Gogh in Amsterdam, by the Musée d'Orsay in Paris, by the Prado in Madrid, and by Basil Blackshaw in Antrim, whose barns and horses and dogs shook me up and stood me on my head. And now in New York I was meeting Picasso, Matisse, Mirò, Rothko, Johns, de Kooning and a load of Pollocks that had me eating my nonexistent hat. A little sculpture of a dog by Giacometti prompted a card to Basil. Woof!

Sometimes I meet people who talk such bull about art (and everything else) that I just say nothing and adopt my rural gobshite Paddy Kavanagh pose. What would *I* know about it? I'm from Philadelphia, says Annie Hall. I'm a hapless culchie, says I. Go away, says I. And these people are everywhere! They call art galleries 'spaces' and they use strange words with abandon. Here I make a list of such words that I must some day look up in a dictionary to find out once and for all what they mean: ersatz, *Zeitgeist*, exegesis, dialectic, chthonic, mainland, triglyph.

My father taught me to draw and paint – horses, faces, proportions – and best of all how to draw people moving – running, kicking a ball, sword-fighting. Men had broader shoulders than women. Women had wider hips. You had to know a bit about anatomy to do it right – the shape of the skull and the bones of the hand. And when you drew a figure you couldn't leave anything out, even the embarrassing bits, the buttocks and the breasts. Women had breasts and everybody had buttocks. You had to look properly at what you were drawing and use a soft pencil. I thought 'buttocks' was a sniggery, uneasy word.

Out once more in the weather, I had a soup-to-go from a deli and began again to tramp through the slush in very damp shoes. There had been a slight thaw and huge icicles were falling like flying glass from windowsills and smashing on the sidewalks below as people ran for cover. Awnings were collapsing under the weight of melting snow and the rumour was that it wouldn't clear until the spring. It was bright, sunny, silent and truly beautiful. Once more the feeling that I did not want to go back to Belfast, the Lagan and the bull. Pass the lotus, please.

Going to study in Belfast in the first place had never been the plan. I had only seen the place once and that was on a trip to visit a schoolmate who was in the Royal Victoria Hospital. It was a horrible, wet and wintery night and one of the priests rounded up a few of us and drove up the motorway to the city. He drove very fast and pointed out the floodlit sky over Long Kesh. It all seemed to confirm that Belfast was a hard and frightening place, the stuff of its own depressing television dramas. Apart from visiting my sick schoolmate, all I remembered of the city were the empty streets, the dim Lucozade glow of the street lamps and the strange violet darkness that hung so heavy on the place. An old bewildered man stopped us in the grounds of the hospital. He was drenched, upset and looking for the maternity ward. I had never seen a place so desolate and unwelcoming.

I had intended going to Trinity and I had been to Dublin many times for day trips, sporting occasions, and in later

years rock concerts at the RDS. I loved Dublin. It smelt of
pastries and coffee and stout and the girls at the bus stops
were beautiful. Near time I got a job there.

My very first trip to Dublin was in Mark McGrath's
Triumph Herald when I was about six or seven. Mark was
my godfather and it was the longest journey in the world.
As we came into the city, he turned and said, 'You're in the
big smoke now.'

We stopped outside the Custom House and there for the
first time I saw a ship. I saw a man with a turban. I saw a
Chinese woman. We walked about all day and my father
went to the Hugh Lane Gallery to look at the paintings. I
looked for the bullet holes on the statue of Daniel
O'Connell and we went to the zoo on a big green
double-decker bus. Elephants, gibbons and a hippopota-
mus. The Phoenix Park. The president's house.

And so Dublin had always been attractive and, like
Donegal, it wasn't the North and there was no shooting
and bombing and tit for tat. But having without much
thought or design got the grades to study law, I had my
arm twisted and was advised to go to Queen's in Belfast.
The law degree, I was told, was a good one. They can't take
it off you et cetera. So I crammed onto an Ulsterbus with
the rest of them and a long Odyssean journey through ice
and snow and every hole in the hedge deposited me finally
in a dark Belfast – Sandy Row to be exact – right at the
door of the Rangers Supporters' Club.

I was the first in my immediate family to go to university
and the whole idea was as strange to my parents as it was
to me. Between the three of us we had no prior inside
knowledge, no connections and no pedigree – I didn't even
know how to get to the university. No chance of me being
chauffeured to my new home in an Audi stuffed with extra

bedclothes and things called duvets. No chance, either, of being left in the care of a procession of older brothers, all high-flyers in the Student Law Society who would ease my entry with tips and recommendations. I was completely on my own in this and I reckoned that the best policy was to tag along, at least at the start, and our ragged band of refugees headed up University Road with bin bags full of sheets, towels and the last properly ironed shirts we would ever see.

These were the mid-eighties, a time of rampant Thatcherism and cuts in most of the areas of society she claimed not to believe in. Education was taking a hammering and yet students could not bring themselves to properly protest.

— NO IFS! NO BUTS! STOP THE EDUCATION CUTS!

Looking back on it, there wasn't much genuine idealism, humour or passion. There were, of course, exceptions but I had the sense early on that I was growing up in the beaten generation. That it was Northern Ireland made things twice as complicated and infinitely more depressing.

Students' Union meetings were, roughly speaking, split down the middle. On the right you had the young Conservative, unionist, heterosexual friends of the Contras, and on the left you had the Marxist, republican, homosexual friends of the Sandinistas. Abuse flew across the room and 'scum' was a favourite word. Brainy bigots are a scary phenomenon. The politics of the place was typically unsophisticated and at times unbelievable as young Tories called for education cuts, while on the left everybody fell so easily into the tabloid stereotype that they were their own worst enemies. Too many marches and not enough marchers.

It was a circus. I remember when the Anglo-Irish

agreement was ceremoniously set alight on one side of the hall and promptly put out by somebody on the other. That done, the young unionist with the Maguire & Patersons was himself put out for causing a fire hazard. An extinguished gentleman, somebody jeered.

But it was all far too grave to laugh at and on the periphery of being far too real. An uncomfortable, hopeless, claustrophobic situation where the narrow view was acceptable and the bunkers well populated. Idealism foundered early. Having said that, I still bought Nicaraguan coffee, wore my COAL NOT DOLE badge, boycotted South African goods and was present when the McMordie Hall in the Students' Union was renamed after Nelson Mandela. I seem to remember that there was a suggestion during that debate that the hall should be renamed after Arthur Scargill, but Mandela swung it. Katmandu then played 'Free Nelson Mandela' six times in a row in the bottom bar.

Northern Ireland had just come through a very tense period. The Hunger Strikes had once again brought the place to boiling point. Older students spoke like veterans who had ridden out this period and survived. One told me that he just stayed in the bar and remained drunk for weeks. He was serious. Things have to be dealt with somehow.

I was beginning to realise just how strange Belfast is, how absurd Belfast is as it loses its general air of menace the very second we take solace in each other's carelessness and the very instant we take comfort in each other. An inspiring humanity just one stagger away from legless desperation. You'll see something similar in any New York Irish bar on a Friday night and it's frightening. Total wipeout.

For some, arriving at university had been a huge trauma but a trauma that brought with it moments of great personal liberation. Coming from a well-integrated town, being in what is called 'mixed company' was never a problem for me, rather a source of a weird and creative energy that might one day get us out of our problems. But for others, being suddenly thrown into the stew was difficult and unbalancing and this instant integration seemed as problematic as your average lecture in tort. Some disintegrated in confusion.

It may seem strange but there were characters arriving at Queen's at the age of eighteen or nineteen who were all of a sudden experiencing their very first encounter with that dreaded person with two heads from the other side. What's more, that other person might be beside you in the canteen, in the tutorial, in the lecture, in the pub, or even under the duvet. Some coped well and showed great imagination and generosity and their faces visibly brightened as the veils dropped away. Others found the challenge too much and too upsetting. It all raised too many questions about what they firmly believed, questions which were far too dangerous to address, and usually they ran blindly into the arms of political or religious groupings waiting to scoop them up. All the hopeless bigots back in their bunkers again, home from home, where they could be themselves, say what they liked and get away with the completely unacceptable as they festered gloomily on.

The rest of us created our own cocoons for reasons of self-preservation. Great big couldn't-care-less bubbles where we could all live regardless of what went on on the campus or on the street. Again life had to be lived skilfully and with tact, but friendships were made and pleasure was pursued with such cross-community spirit that we should have got a grant for it.

Many of us hadn't a care in the world, had no idea where we were going, and did not feel particularly concerned. Other students, however, seemed to have their life plan already worked out and were solely intent on getting degree, job, house, car, spouse and golf club membership in no particular order. In the Faculty of Law many of the girls wore business clothes, many of the boys wore tweed, and most of them tried to sit at the front.

One of the first pieces I wrote for radio while still at Queen's, some ten years ago, was a lament for lost youth which put the boot into these people old before their time. As I read it now I'm pleased to see that even then my healthy cynicism was starting to get rather ill.

All anyone ever has to show for themselves after university is a bit of paper which is often useless. The important thing is surely to emerge as your own man or your own woman, fit to do things in your own way, and be able to cook up a good chilli con carne when called upon. You should have stories to tell your grandchildren and, more importantly, stories you wouldn't dare tell your grandchildren. Students these days seem to be studying the *Financial Times* and investing in South African companies and talking about personal pensions. What sort of perverted behaviour is this for young people? A yuppie is not as it sounds, some harmless, cuddly, furry creature from Tolkien. A yuppie is a horrible, disgusting and evil thing. But thanks to economics, they'll never last.

Badly written, crude, during the apartheid era, before BSE, before I had a pension plan, and full of a passionate anger which does not embarrass me as much as the writing. The only reason it still exists is that on the back of the script there is a tangle of strange, scrawly signatures – the fancy autographs of footballers, most of them impossible to make out. The night I broadcast this attack on my fellow students was the same night as George Best's testimonial at Windsor Park. I wasn't at the match but I was at the Europa and I'm pleased that despite my crude cynicism and very bad hairstyle, I still had enough of my childhood in me to get the autographs of Ruud Krol, Paul Breitner, Liam Brady, Johan Neeskens, Matt Busby and, of course, George Best.

Georgie Best, superstar,
Wears frilly knickers and he wears a bra.

So the cool police hadn't interned me yet. Neither had the style cops. The photographic evidence is frightening. Stripy trousers, sleeveless T-shirts with Chinese writing, a studded belt. All of that plus the long hair and I looked like something out of an awful American heavy metal band. Thankfully that changed as I devoted more time to Coltrane, Dylan, Morrison and Muddy. Rush and Deep Purple started to get a bit silly and I began, ever so slowly, to catch myself on. I had been listening to all kinds of music from my last years at school. I used to get records out of the library at home, like *The Stardust Session* by John Coltrane. An album like that was big enough to dwell in and, listening to it, I regularly went off into some kind of sleepy, hallucinatory trance, listening perhaps to only one instrument at a time, Red Garland's piano or Jimmy Cobb's drums. Yet another planet.

And then I saw a documentary about Coltrane where the drummer Elvin Jones said that he believed enough to say, in all seriousness, that John Coltrane was an angel. I was

moved by this and slightly awakened to the possibility that
life was not as compartmentalised as education had led me
to believe. For instance, there was the immediate and
straightforward revelation that God's music is jazz. 'Faith
of Our Fathers', fair enough, but what about 'A Love
Supreme'? Here at last a real opening up of the head and
another angle on everything.

I was beginning to realise that there were more
approaches to life than the ones I had been offered. I was
beginning to see that the philosophies I had been lumbered
with were narrow and limiting (at least in their current
alignment) and that Monaghan clerics would never be
enough. There were big questions to be addressed and I
was only starting to realise, with joy, what some of those
liberating questions were, never mind the answers to them.
I was eighteen and it was near time.

The first Morrison record I heard was *Saint Dominic's
Preview* and that certainly opened the ears further. Dylan
took longer, but Freddy King, B.B. King, Muddy Waters
and John Lee Hooker were immediate. The tapes were all
in the sports bag as I walked from Sandy Row, up
University Road, past Queen's and up the Malone to the
halls of residence – late nights, jazz and instant coffee made
with Marvel.

But for all the hints at wisdom and the teasing glimpses
of understanding, we were a right collection of eejits,
victims as well as beneficiaries of this new freedom. Some
took to boozing in a dangerous way, others in a bog
standard student way. I'm not sure what I did but I
certainly looked stupid and lived in various ridiculous
boxes. Not a clue. Not a baldy's notion. Fantasy Island.

In the halls of residence there was no need to tie the
school tie around your head to act the lad. Now it was a

better idea to have a guitar in the corner of the room and a few well-chosen books. English students always banged on about Larkin but I thought he was a dry sort of fish. I decorated the shelf with Kerouac, Hunter S. Thompson and Tom Wolfe. *The Electric Kool-Aid Acid Test*. Predictable enough, but Yeats was in there too and *The Fermanagh Story* – the yellowest book in the world. A little line of cassette tapes added considerably to the room's effect. Tom Waits, Leonard Cohen, Van Morrison, Bob Dylan and Billie Holiday. If a woman didn't respond to any of that I reckoned there was no point in pursuing things anyway. Ever since Moving Hearts in Bundoran, I took it for granted that women just didn't like good music. They were all into Dire Straits and Chris de Burgh and I had accepted this as a sad reality. Then in second year I met someone who was into Morrison, Elvis Costello, Coltrane and Mozart, and we were together for years.

Music and books were very important. It was all a sort of coded kit to identify yourself to like-minded people. There was no need to have a personality of your own. The contents of your room would cut through all preliminaries and give you a head start. You *were* your record collection, and maybe this still applies. And is it really possible to love someone who doesn't love Ella Fitzgerald? I doubt it.

The problem, of course, is that all these accoutrements eventually begin to replace the real person. They become a sort of stage-managed image of yourself and inevitably a better version. If you are an amalgam of Frank Sinatra, Shakespeare and James Dean, then you're quite the guy. Ask any intelligent rock star, any actor who isn't a megalomaniac, any famous person who hates his or her condition, and they will tell you that image is a killer. I've since seen people destroyed by it. Certainly I've seen others thrive on it but they too are, sure as shootin', doomed. In the end, the projector will crank down and the reels will run backwards and the film will spill all about their boots and leave them as nude as a bee.

And so I knock the writing on the head for a while, conscious that I might be getting into a rant, getting wound up about all the bullshit at home when I should be full of New York craziness. I take the rest of the early hours off and lie on the bed in the glow of the television. And then a stroke of luck – *Casablanca*. A hill of beans. *De minimis non curat lex*.

16

Next morning in a Broadway diner the notebook was out and the bagels were hot. I went at it furiously, wanting to finish it and put it under the bed. I was finding very little in my time at university other than typical student antics and a sense of it being a kind of Disneyland.

I was also mad to get into what followed Queen's. Work, job, and all that went with it, and I was saving all of that up like a last white knuckle cigarette. Also, if I got something substantial done, I'd feel all right about heading to Brooklyn with Rossa. Clear conscience. Work ethic.

The waiter was the roundest man I had ever seen and he seemed to roll up and down behind the counter like a bowling ball.

— More coffee? You writing a blockbuster, kid? Make
sure there's plenty of sex in it!

For some reason I remembered a song we used to sing in
the cub scouts.

You'll never get to heaven with Brigitte Bardot
'Cos Brigitte Bardot is going below.

I didn't know who Brigitte Bardot was but she must have
been a bad woman, like the man who killed Maria Goretti
was a bad man. Those were very confusing days and I
hadn't a clue. Not like university where we knew it all, or
to be more accurate, we thought we knew it all. No French
vamps gallivanting in Belmore Street. No Brigitte Bardot
looking after a thousand cats like Lily Chapman, throwing
crusts to a white tornado of seagulls on the bridge.

— Show me what you're writing, kid.
— No, it's nothing.
— Ah go on, kid, I'm getting real curious.
I turned the page around and the spherical waiter
inclined his head, as if to cog.
— You'll never get to heaven with Brigitte Bardot!
He began to chuckle gently.
— You kiddin' me, kid? What you writing about
anyway? You FBI or somethin'?
— No, I'm writing about Queen's –
— Queens! Shit! This town's a freak show! Freaks
everywhere!
I put the man right and he gave me more coffee.
— It must have been a strange place to grow up, eh kid?
Northern I-yerland?
— Ah, not so bad – as far as I can remember it anyway.

— Ah the days beyond recall, he said, days beyond recall.

Queen's (the university) remained a cocoon, sealed from Belfast and from the awful events that continued to happen hundreds of yards away. Locked up in the bottom bar for folk nights or blues nights or the bedlam encouraged by the Bavarian Beerstompers, we partied middling to hard. Katmandu continued to provide the score to the chaos of that time – sleeping all day, out all night, missing lectures and photocopying other people's notes. The osmosis principle – and it seemed to work. Worry about it later and then there was always Saint Jude, and Kieran Goss in the Speakeasy singing 'Is She Really Going Out with Him?' and Paul Brady in the Mandela singing 'Crazy Dreams'.

Law was incredibly dull at times and sometimes seemed to amount to learning for the sake of it. Memorising very complicated sections and subsections and exceptions to subsections, all just to demonstrate that you could do it. I always thought that what I was engaged in was about as useful as learning off the telephone directory when a more sensible approach might simply be to keep it beside the phone. But I don't make the rules and you can't beat city hall. The subject and the concept were treated with such reverence by some that it was like learning the sacred rites of some mystical sect.

I was for the most part bored out of my head and it took several rather eccentric lecturers and a few exceptionally kind individuals to provide some light relief from the more passionless and humourless contingent whose only kicks in life seemed to be found in the long-winded decision of Lord Justice somebody in a case not yet reported. Oh, the maddening boredom!

And there's the proof of it! As soon as I start thinking about law I write a sentence that lasts a paragraph. I'll leave it there as boring evidence. Rebut that if you're so smart! That's what the study of law did for me. Ruined my handwriting and screwed up my sentences. You must acquit! Objection! Sustained! Overruled! And which is which?

Another problem for me was that most of my contemporaries were mad keen to be lawyers, and I never shared their enthusiasm. When we visited the courts they lapped it all up – the bowing and conferring and strutting about with piles of law reports. I was always uncomfortable, uneasy with seeing people frightened and nervous, disturbed by handcuffs and sendings down. I was like a medical student who couldn't stand the sight of blood. It was not for me.

Having said that, some of it was a hoot. The lecturer who demonstrated what criminal damage was by smashing the light bulb. The character who treated us regularly to a puppet show and the works of McGonagall.

Beautiful Silv'ry Tay,
With all your landscapes, so lovely and gay,
Along each side of your waters, to Perth all the way;
No other river in the world has got scenery so fine,
Only I am told the beautiful Rhine,
Near to Wormit Bay, it seems very fine.

He and several others made the whole experience much more bearable.

Even so, I thought I envied the English students who were probably getting grilled in Dante and I tried to do an unofficial literature course on the side, secretly reading Kafka and Gogol and Marlowe over a toasted sandwich (burnt plastic and all) and a pint of still orange in the Speakeasy. Better than *Wylie on Irish Land Law* and no exams to sit. But then they had *Beowulf* to contend with. Swings and roundabouts.

I started to write for the student newspaper, concert reviews mainly. The first was Peter Green, then Dave Gilmour, Queen, the Long Ryders, Jason and the Scorchers, the Ramones, Paul Brady, the Pogues, Doctor John, Stevie Wonder and Bob Dylan. I also wrote satirical columns under the names Liam Duck and Terry O'Type and they were full of bad puns and any available weak linguistic joke. In fact, I used to refer to it as my 'weakly' column. It should have been axed.

But there were real writers about, too. The English Society organised readings by the likes of Mario Vargas Llosa and Sorley MacLean. The local brigade of McGuckian, Simmons, Ormsby, Carson and Longley were also in evidence and all provided encouragement to those of us starting to attempt something serious. Poetry, no less. Short stories. In the background was the mysterious figure of Joe (alias Padraic Fiacc) and even further in the background were the sobering influences of McFadden and Hewitt. Poems of mine appeared in the *Irish Press* and the *Honest Ulsterman* and I was very pleased with myself. I thought for a spell that I might be a poet. One of the younger ones. I wrote funny stuff and it got a laugh but, quite rightly, not much else. As Quentin Crisp once remarked, a poet is a terrible thing to happen to anybody.

I don't know whether it was reinvention or wising up, but attitudes very quickly began to change. My girlfriend, who was an enlightened and well-read woman from Derry, provided me with Patrick Kavanagh's *Collected*

Poems and I had an immediate hero. A Monaghan man
who wasn't wearing a collar.

AUTHOR'S NOTE The same man wrote that he disliked
talking about himself in a direct way. He said that the self
was only interesting as an illustration and that whenever
we talk about our personal lives they turn out to be both
irrelevant and untrue. And so, chastened by the Monaghan
man, I move along swiftly.

END OF AUTHOR'S NOTE

Down through France and into Italy and so by boat to
Greece. And up through Greece and out through the
cornfields of Yugoslavia and over to Venice and up to
Salzburg and out to Vienna and on to Moscow and up to
Leningrad and back down to the Black Sea and over to
Germany and Switzerland and Belgium and mad
Amsterdam and down through France and into Spain
and over to Lisbon and up to Donegal.

Cheap travel and Interrail tickets got me around every
summer. Sleeping in train stations and hostels and beaches
and holes in the hedge, under the stars, full of adventure
and starving with hunger. Loaves of bread were bought in
Austria and were still being chewed, dry and stale, in Italy
a week down the road. Water bottles were filled in Zagreb
and Tunisian sandwiches were guzzled, chilli and all, in
Paris. The secret was to travel all night, to sleep on the
train, and in that way dispense with the need for costly
accommodation. Get to the station early, get into a
carriage, hang dirty socks everywhere and be generally
objectionable. This was to keep people out, to make the
carriage so unpleasant that nobody would want to sit in it
and so you'd have room enough to yourself to stretch out

140 in France and waken up in Rome.

It was rough and it was tiresome but it was magical. It was what I'd been after all through those years frustrated by school and the nothingness of a Friday night. Down the town, Forthill Street, pubs full of kids (at least that's how we saw it then) and then New Year's Eve in a shop doorway in the rain with Spud, the final insult. We wrote a song:

We all live in Enniskillen,
The spirit is weak and the flesh is willin'.
We all live in Enniskillen,
We go to the Killy but we like Bob Dylan.

And now suddenly the Latin Quarter, the Barrio Alto, Trastevere. My hair was long and my gutties worn. I was at last the penniless traveller on the lost highway, the road was my middle name and I was your genuine Dharma Bum. Jack Kerouac and now myself. Head-the-ball on tour. Fermanagh man riding the rails down Italia's leg and paying respects to Joyce in Zurich beside the zoo.

I disappeared every summer and came back with ridiculous hair and a weather-beaten face, alive with stories of railway station slumbering, authority dodging and being hosed off the steps of Venice at dawn. It was all about lying out at night and listening to the cicadas and feeling like some romantic hero from a book I hadn't yet written (but plenty of others had). Most of it was reasonably harmless, all the same. The closest run-in with the law was in Monte Carlo and it was innocent enough. My travelling companion was doing a skilled, albeit rather insensitive, impression of Inspector Clouseau outside the police station.

— Eez zat yourh minky? he asked aloud. Douze yourh

dueg baht?

The cop on duty wasn't impressed. Nor was he affected by my weak joke that my friend should be charged with impersonating a police officer. It was almost a tear gas situation and so we left the country. Made a break for the border. I didn't like Monte Carlo anyway. I had no money and looked it and was not welcome anywhere.

— It's closed, announced every waiter. It's finished!

And I would retort with great cosmopolitan sophistication.

— Ah g'way and shite!

(You can take the man out of the bog et cetera.)

Monte Carlo was no place for a skinny long-hair who hadn't seen the sun for a year. Right enough, I *was* frightening looking. Young children tugged at their mothers' hands and pointed. Get me into Italy quick, where the railway guards whistle tunes and the girls at San Remo hang their dresses on bushes at midnight.

And then in October it was back to statutes and law reports and Lord Justice whatever and I wrote poems during lectures. All of them about elsewhere, because that is where all the wonder was. Even so, apart from dealing with a certain amount of tedious study, keeping warm in freezing rented dives and rationing the grant, I had very little to worry about. We were all insulated like decadent monks in a decadent monastery. It was all late nights and cherry blossom. Blackbirds singing, badgers scraping and drunks falling over in the hedge. Carefree and careless. Studenty. But every so often the world *did* come in from over the wall and we could no longer ignore it.

My home town became famous. Television around the world began to refer to Enniskillen as an event rather than a place. Eleven people were killed when my old scout hall collapsed on them. A bomb. There's not much left to say about it now. Enniskillen is a small town and I knew some of those who died. Everybody here knows people who have died and that's exactly the sadness of Northern Ireland. We tell everyone that it's perfectly normal and yet we all know very well that it's very far from it. Determinedly, we live on among the victims like uneasy boozers at a wake.

Back in cuckooland, someone said that university would be like any other relationship. The first year would be wildly exciting, the second year would be comfortable and secure, in the third year you would get itchy and by the fourth year you wouldn't be able to stand the sight of the place.

When the cherry tree blossomed again, it was the signal that sent me briefly to the books. It was hard to study but I dug in for the final memory test. Frantic photocopying and searching for better-written and comprehensible books which might explain what had been going on in certain lectures that had slowly devoured vital hours of cool fleshy spring.

I worked in final year, got a decent degree and found myself faced with a head-bealding year at the grandly titled Institute of Professional Legal Studies. Another year when I wouldn't have to do anything particularly serious, just get it over with. And anyway, I certainly didn't have any better ideas. Except perhaps to bum around Paris (which I did just as soon as I got loose).

So there I was, five years on and no further on. My friends scattered to their new posts in awful places, my girlfriend vanished, and I found myself, as I believe AE once said about Yeats, like an umbrella left behind after a party. Stranded. Marooned. Snowed in.

We dug Rossa's car out of the snow on Seventh Avenue and drove like maniacs to Brooklyn. Down through Alphabet City and out over the bridge that makes me think of Drogheda and 'Madame George'.

— Mind that skier! Watch!

— I met Vanessa Williams the other night.

— For God's sake, man, slow down, you'll hit that horse!

— She was real nice. Did you go to Letterman?

— Yeah. It was – slow down – I was talking to Mujibar.

— What about Rupert G?

— Man, he does great soup. Letterman's a hoot!

— You still working in television?

— I do and I don't.

— Is your show like Letterman's?

— I don't have a show. Slow down, will you!

— I thought you had a TV show?

— I used to.

— What happened?

— They put me under a pedestal.

— A what?

— A pedestal. Under a pedestal.

— Woody Allen, right?

— Right!

— Did you see him?

— Yeah, the other night. He's a quare boy.

— A what?

— A quare fella.

— Oh yes, *The Quare Fellow*! I think my dad knew Brendan Behan. What's your book about?

— Don't ask me. Are we here yet?

— Was he good?

— Who?

— Woody Allen.

— Brilliant! He played that song 'The Sun Shone Bright on Charlie Chaplin'.

— What?

— Charlie Chaplin. Send him off to the Dardanelles. There's another name for it – he did that – big banjo player sang it!

— Was he good?

— Great! He did 'Ain't Gonna Give Nobody None of My Jelly Roll' and 'Easter Bonnet'.

— Can't hear you.

— Slow down! Jelly Roll!

— They put you under a pedestal?

— You're damn right! Are we here yet?

Another neighbourhood dark and piled with snow. Rossa's friends Gian and Helen cooked me a beefburger that is lying in my stomach to this day and I was given executive control over a let-me-have-it record collection bought entirely at garage sales. The musical menu I believe was as follows: Tex Ritter, Curtis Mayfield, Slim Gaillard and Johnny Cash, and then I gave my usual long-winded lecture on life before Elvis.

— There were guys like Roy Brown and Wynonie Harris ... blah, blah, blah.

Another mad journey back.

— You ever read Hunter Thompson?

— Yes.

— What's Vanessa Williams like?

— What's your radio programme on?

— Its last legs. I'm baling out.

I disembarked as soon as we landed back in Manhattan. Rossa was to meet some rich woman who wanted him to accompany her to Vietnam or Indonesia or somewhere just to take pictures. She lived around Battery Park, and I

walked up to Tower Records on Broadway at Fourth Street
and bought up the shop. Little Jimmy Scott, Garnet
Mimms, Irma Thomas, Duke Ellington. They were playing
the Jive Five on the public address. Where else would you
get it?

On the long tramp up Broadway there was a tune going
around in my head. Bobby Short at the Café Carlyle
singing 'I Happen to Like New York'.

— Good evening, Café Carlyle.
— How ya doin'? Is Bobby Short on the night, is he?
— I'm afraid not, sir.
— I happen to like New York! I happen to like New
York! I happen to like New York!

— Good evening, Sweet Basil.
— How ya doin'? Who's on the night?
— Nat Adderley and his quintet, sir.
— Right enough? Is he?
— Absolutely, sir.
— Is Jimmy Cobb with him?
— Yes, sir. He's at the bar right now.
— Right. I'll be down in a minute.

17

I sat up late, one eye on the television and one eye on the present. The room was a mess, the office of some Dickensian lawyer and there but for the grace of God et cetera. The more I thought about my present state, incarnation, life, job and function, the more I realised that there was little to say that could be said. I wanted to write about being three years old again. That's all I could remember and so the hotel paper filled up with frantic, idle doodles. Hook-nosed faces. Ears. Fish. Hares. Boxes and more boxes. Hooks. Boxes. Giant barbed fishing hooks. Boxes. And where would I find a shrink at this time of night?

I began to work it all out. The reason I had made all

those decadent bolts for Saint-Germain or London (during my Blue Period) had been to escape the alleged big smoke of Belfast and my alleged successes and failures within it. But surely I knew this all along, even when I was doing it? And then that sudden odd sensation of realising something you had already realised. It makes you feel both clear-headed and stupid. The obvious is a wonderful light bulb.

And the cod rhyme I wrote on one of my rakish Paddy jaunts to London, on the back of a matchbox from a Chelsea restaurant:

I vanish when I'm in the mood,
A little jaunt to clear the head.
Mini-bars and king-size beds
Are certain cures for multitude.

Later that London night, crossing the bridge back towards the Barbican, I met someone I knew under cardboard crazy paving. We recognised each other at once. Down and out. Over and out. Me ranting on the wireless, spoofing on the telly covered in orange make-up, getting recognised in the street in another way entirely.

It appeared that I now had what you might call a career working in television and radio. It raised many questions and I took advice from others. Derek Bell of the Chieftains introduced me to Van Morrison and we became kind of pals round about this time. We went out for grub and talked for hours about life and music and it was a hoot. I learnt much from him about the realities of celebrity, fame, so-called success and Cockney rhyming slang. I saw close up what it means to be in the public eye, and it's never a bowl of cherries. Not that anyone believes it. Most people refuse with absolute determination to believe that any amount of notoriety can mean anything other than total happiness. The same way that people refuse to believe that actors don't do their own stunts, people seem to have a need to believe what is evidently untrue, and all of this gets projected onto 'stars'. Fortunately, *hubris* is something instinctively understood by Fermanagh people (so is *nemesis*) and the *hubris* detector is always left switched on just in case.

I was uneasy in my new media swim, surrounded and suddenly the focus of some strangely driven people whose agendas I would never value or aspire to. Cliques and lobbies and jealous scribes who, as a poet once said, herded their myopic angers and yet could never deny him his place.

But then there were the others. All the greats about Belfast who welcomed new arrivals into their world – David Hammond, Joe McPartland, Raymond Piper, Neil Shawcross, Solly Lipsitz, Joe McWilliams, Basil Blackshaw – people who encouraged and shared. And the notes and postcards from others long gone from the North, people you were always so very glad to see, old heroes and old friends. I would have been lost without them and they helped me and many others to keep the faith.

In a crisis of faith, however, celebrity, myth and back-stabbing became my small hours rant. Broken record, bitter, half-baked stuff only properly focused when I read a book by Artie Shaw called *The Trouble with Cinderella*. I had bought it in the Blue Note on West Third Street the last time I had been in New York. Shaw wrote it in 1952 after he'd had his fill of being the clarinet-playing band leader and big-time star of the swing era. He had been hugely successful as musician, band leader and composer but all of a sudden, as Woody Herman put it, he decided to make

a lamp out of his clarinet. He knocked it all on the head
and decided to work out exactly what was going on and
who exactly he was. Who was Arthur Arshawsky now that
he had realised that chasing what he had been after was
like 'kissing a buzz-saw'? He retells the tale of a poor girl in
the cinders who is rescued from her ugly sisters (a couple
of beat-up crows) by the handsome prince. They, of course,
live happily ever after. Shaw then takes it further and asks
what 'happy ever after' actually means. In one move the
pitiful Cinders has achieved a happy marriage, wealth,
social position, prestige and so on – what is known as
success. She gets what she has been wishing for. The book
looks at how Cinderella was then likely to fare in her new
set-up. Would she get along with the king and queen?
With prime ministers and their wives? What about
children? What about the prince away all the time killing
dragons? What if she got bored? Irritated? Trapped?
Unhappy? The biggest problem, however, as Artie Shaw
points out, is that Cinderella is *never* going to tell you, even
if she understands it herself. As they say in South Carolina,
'We ain't what we wanna be and we ain't what we're
gonna be – but we ain't what we was.'

It's a great book. I read it every so often myself and I
loan it out to people who need it. It has cured a few
musicians. Not for nothing was Artie Shaw's theme tune
an ominous and edgy number called 'Nightmare' – hard to
dance to, but perfect nonetheless. He had his head screwed
on.

Footballers had been there all through primary school,
rock stars had been there during St Mick's, writers had
been there during Queen's and now in the workplace my
new heroes were all musicians, most of them long dead.
Charlie Parker, Robert Johnson, Hank Williams, Johnny

Ace. And yes, despite my own protestations about fame and myth, I fall for it too.

CHARLIE PARKER Supernatural genius yardbird who drank and drugged himself to death. Played with his eyes open. Spoke with a posh accent. 'Relaxing at Camarillo'.

ROBERT JOHNSON Sold his soul to the devil. Crossroads. Two photographs. Died on his knees barking like a dog. Poison? The devil? Genius. 'Hellhound on my Trail'.

HANK WILLIAMS New Year's Day 1953 died in the back of the car. Drinking, painkillers. Genius. 'I'm So Lonesome I Could Cry'.

JOHNNY ACE The late great Johnny Ace. One album. Posthumous. Christmas Eve. Russian roulette. 'Pledging My Love'.

This entanglement of myth and reality is irresistible. I admit I went a bit wobbly myself one surreal night at the Dundonald Ice Bowl near Belfast when I looked Bob Dylan in the eye and we shook hands. I know every word of his songs and his music has been important to me, so it was a strange experience to be in his company. Uncle Bob – a straw hat, a whole go of snazzy shirts and very long fingernails.

Businessmen they drink my wine.

It became ever more apparent that university had been a bubble, an insulated situation where you can be whatever you want to be but not necessarily who you actually are. I had been the star of my very own movie and now the wrap had been called. Cast, supporting cast and extras had all scattered and I was left not quite sure what my role had been or even what kind of movie I had been in. My new role as minor local celebrity could well have dragged me further and further away from my real self if I had let it. All I knew for sure was that, like Saint Patrick, I had come from decent people.

And so I sought refuge there. I became increasingly drawn to my own ones, straining to see cartwrights, carpenters, fishermen, tailors, maids, dressmakers, electricians, bakers, people who worked in pubs, in fields, in solicitors' offices and in the bookies. Home was the only constant, the only dependable world, free of pathetic intrigue and where the throwing of shapes would be met with precision ridicule and a brutal slagging.

The solution seemed obvious but it simply wasn't practical. I could not just go home. South Carolina once again. And so the old policy of tearing the arse out of everything. Always making the joke. Always deflating and never on any account being too serious. People might laugh at you. People might slag you off. People might think you were getting above yourself. Getting too smart. Too fancy. Too much like a writer or an actor or one of them other playboys. It's a common condition and I've got a dose of it. It can be a good thing because I've seen the results of its absence, the sort of people who pontificate about piles of bricks in the Tate Gallery. The people who slabber about Marshall McLuhan in cinema queues. It can be a bad thing because it holds you back, all that reticence we're so well-reared on. Standing back, self-protective hanging back, never blowing our own trumpets, only our own whistles. Constantly putting ourselves down so that we might look less rattled when someone else does it – and without question, someone else will. It's all part of that Graeco-Fermanagh *hubris/nemesis* business.

There was another imaginative world and this was the

one in which I often preferred to live. It was America and all my buddies lived there – Muddy, Lightnin', Wynonie, Brother Ray, Bird and Lady Day. My obsession with black American music grew and I took to reading Langston Hughes, James Baldwin, Amiri Baraka (LeRoi Jones) and Mezz Mezzrow, a white man who thought he was black. I got stuck into heavy texts on blues and jazz and became an amateur student of American social and cultural history (pre-Elvis). At times I talked the language. It was like joining a comfortable gang, this time dead black Americans with high-waisted trousers and kipper ties. Parker, Coltrane, Monk and the rest were all extraordinary and they came to symbolise individuality, integrity and creativity, all the qualities which were beginning to be less and less desirable in our dogma-driven, cynical and soul-less workplaces. My heroes, therefore, had to be heroic, extraordinary, subversive and even supernatural. Real people.

I played their records on the radio and the right people responded. Old R & B acts who had been ripped off by the squeaky-clean white versions. I played the Chords and never the Crew Cuts, Little Richard and never Pat Boone. I tried to do the right thing, and again the right people responded. We took sides with Arthur Crudup, Willie Dixon and Chuck Berry. It was the right side and no regrets. We had a big glittery day out in London when the show won a thing called an award. I found myself in the vicinity of Tony Blackburn and Jimmy Saville, the man who fixes it, and I realised that yet another absurd turning point had been arrived at.

I haven't yet worked out the personal implications of this media lark. When I do, I'll have to come back to New York to write the book. I think I'd enjoy that. I'd call it

'White Knuckles' and spill the hill of beans. Might do me
some good.

Inside my own head I moved shop to America. With my
university friends for the most part living somewhere else,
the thought of burrowing into a packed Belfast pub became
less and less appealing and my preference became the
lonely freakish voice of Little Jimmy Scott or to watch
again my Manhattan companions on video: Ike, Dale,
Tracy, Emily, Mary and her ex-husband Jeremiah. The
opening shots – Brooklyn Bridge, Elaine's, Central Park,
the Guggenheim, Park Avenue, Radio City Music Hall – so
far from my other worlds and yet no distance. Gershwin
and fireworks.

The imaginative world was thriving and well-populated
and inspired by it I continued to footer about with words. I
wrote a novel about a diabolic pact. I was at the crossroads.
I read Artie Shaw's book again and listened to Robert
Johnson in the middle of the night.

I realised that it was time once again to lie down in my
own field and breathe nothing but my own natural
atmosphere. A skyful of herons. A loughful of bream.
The silence when the outboard dies and the echoing sonar
of the water hen. The bubbling curlews, the snipe and the
lapwing rising and tumbling over meadows. A field alive
with larks and hares – big, crazy, leaping, red, Irish hares.
Pat Lunny's boat up to Sandy Bottom, strip off and swim.
Total immersion.

And so the Devenish Empire State Lough Erne Hudson
River Syndrome from which I gladly suffer. Big-eared
Kellys waving down at Fred Astaire. The Island. Woody
Allen playing 'We Shall Not Be Moved' in Michael's pub.
Rushes. Tonystick. Topped Mountain. Big Paris. The

154 | Golden Arrow. Blakes of the Hollow. Peggy the Bull's Lane. Kipperlugs. The jukebox in P.J. Clarke's. Rooney's Path. The Broad Meadow. Rossa's car roaring into Brooklyn. The Forthill. Nat Adderley. Herons. Broadway. Bagels. Pete Hamill's apartment for grub. Greenwich Village.

18

And while all of this was going on in Belfast et cetera, the planet earth was still revolving away blah, blah, blah...

Glasnost, the Anglo-Irish agreement, Tienanmen Square, Thatcher Out, the Berlin Wall, Romania, the Velvet Revolution, Nelson Mandela, Baghdad, bombs, murder, Riverdance...

And then suddenly – ceasefire.

19

I was flicking through Michael Pye's book *Maximum City: A Biography of New York*. An interesting passage on the natural history of the city informed me that the garter snakes and the brown snakes have vanished. The wild pigeons that tasted of partridge have all been shot. All manner of lizards and strange beasts have been let loose in the parks. The snapper turtle scares the citizens as it hauls itself out onto the bank. The sparrow and the starling have taken over and the pink ladyslipper orchid is cared for in tiny patches of the Bronx. I informed Raymond Piper by postcard (no more passenger pigeons). He'll know the proper name for it.

The Lower East Side was like the Bering Strait, half-frozen, half-open ocean, and it was snowing hard again. I jumped from floe to floe, sidewalk to sidewalk, and finally shook the snow off my hat in the elevator to Pete and Fukiko's apartment. I was soaking, sneezing and spluttering, a drowneded rat out of the East River. We talked about Belfast and our uneasy peace. We talked about Mexico. We talked about the night Pete spent driving around the empty wet streets of New York in the back of Frank Sinatra's limousine and I was fairly certain that I couldn't think of anybody else I knew who was on first-name terms with Uncle Frank. Or with Muhammad Ali, for that matter, and here Pete donated the mother of all anecdotes.

Pete and Muhammad Ali are driving to Norman Mailer's house and Ali spots a little man out in his driveway fixing a tyre.

— Stop the car! Ali suddenly commands.

He gets out, stands over the man and taps him on the shoulder. The man turns, looks up and, quite naturally, drops the wheel brace. His mouth hangs open as Ali towers over him, raises his fists, bares his teeth, bites his lower lip and hisses.

— You wanna fight? You wanna fight?

The man slumps to the ground. Ali gets back in the car in hysterics and remarks that for the rest of his life that man will tell his neighbours that Muhammad Ali had challenged him to a fight – and that nobody will ever believe him.

Perhaps that is the greatest joy of New York. It connects you to everything. Muhammad Ali. The rumble in the jungle. Kinshasa, Zaïre, 30 October 1974. The starry television picture, the faint commentary, and Ali on the ropes. The terror that he might lose. George Foreman's haymakers and then Ali suddenly off the ropes and all over in the eighth. Ali! Floats like a butterfly! The greatest! And in a club in Louisville, Kentucky, my buddy Sid Griffin is just a kid and all his buddies are hiding in cupboards as Ali comes in through the kitchen to see Ike and Tina Turner. Wide-eyed, they peer out at the greatness.

Pete listened patiently as I tried to articulate my feelings about the city in which I had been living for twelve years. At times recently the place had become unbearable, and for the first time in my conscious memory it had been hopeless and terrifying. The radio show had been interrupted too many times by news bulletins and news flashes of death and massacre. Scattered chairs, bloodstains, bombs, limbs, getaway cars, pillion passengers and screaming relatives. It had been hard to follow the news with a Louis Prima record – hard to follow the news with anything. The obvious thought was always: you only live once, so why live in Belfast?

And then things changed all of a sudden and we began to hold our breath in hope. The shooting stopped and there were no soldiers at the border. Strange and unthinkable things were happening. There was talk of peace, a peace process, a settlement, talks and no more war. Andy White and Liam Ó Maonlaí were in the Warehouse and I got up with the tin sandwich to jam and hyperventilate on a Sonny Boy song. Liam sang a Joe Dolan song for the laugh and Andy sang 'Na Na Na Na'. At midnight, the second of two ceasefires came into operation. Candles were lit, everyone said some kind of furtive prayer and into that room full of booze, cigarette smoke and rock-'n'-roll, the Holy Ghost most definitely came down through the roof.

When I left Pete and Fukiko I was once again in a wonderful New York spin. Belfast. Sinatra. Muhammad

Ali. Ceasefires and good company. Are you a Catlick or a Prodesan? I'm a boy! I went home via Bradley's on University Place and listened to Ray Drummond, Gary Bartz and Idris Muhammad. Ray swayed like his own metronome and the music got me right in the heart. So happy. So content. It was my last night and, as ever, I did *not* want to go home. Another lotus fruit, please.

The snow was soft and heavy as I took a late night walk in the miraculous. The sky was purple and the whole city was deserted, silent and cushioned in whiteness. There was no traffic and no people and I drifted alone through the dunes of snow, shivering in the magic of it all. And then suddenly Barry Flanagan's hares came to life on Park Avenue and ran full tilt through the freezing air. Leaping, tumbling, scurrying, flying and rearing up to box the traffic lights that said WALK – DON'T WALK to nobody. Big bronze trickster hares come alive and frantic on their own crisscross snowy Manhattan pads. Their secret late night madness up the walls, the lamp-posts, the skyscrapers, and across from block to block, high and out of sight in the violet snowy sky.

I sat on the bonnet of a buried Cadillac and watched them for an hour – just myself – alone in the echoey canyon of Park Avenue. I had all New York to myself and soon the hares came close. They sat about me, one here, one there, another over there, and we blessed each other with our silence. They knew me well from home, my real home and my real place. They'd seen me standing in the middle of them many times before – on the mossy rock, in the middle of the meadow, in the middle of the Island, in the middle of the lough. And so I bowed to them again, my magic, leaping hares who have always been and always will be there, regardless.

The cab ride to the airport was a lonesome one as I savoured the last of the Manhattan skyline. I had only been away a week, and snowbound airport permitting, I would soon be back in Belfast with a book to deliver and a million scraps of paper to decipher. It had been, for me, a kind of island retreat – a decadent Lough Derg, a frantic Devenish. I had contemplated myself in solitude high in a Fifty-seventh Street hotel and I had cleansed myself in multitude in the life-giving madness of tumbling avenues and blizzard. I had, in the end, discovered something definite about myself. As I believe John Cage has already declared: I have nothing to say and I am saying it.

Ich bin ein Fermanagh man.